W9-BCR-391

CPS-Morrill School Library

34880 00010479 9

Haque, Jameel   954.91 HAQ
Pakistan

DATE DUE

954.91
HAQ   Haque, Jameel
           Pakistan

           Morrill School Library
           Chicago Public Schools
           6011 S. Rockwell
           Chicago, IL 60629

COUNTRIES OF THE WORLD

Pakistan

Gareth Stevens Publishing
A WORLD ALMANAC EDUCATION GROUP COMPANY

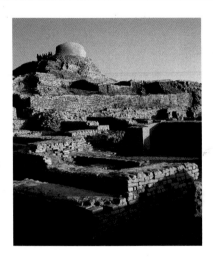

About the Author: Jameel Haque is a Pakistani-American whose father is from Pakistan. Born and raised in New York, Haque has a degree in psychology from Drew University, New Jersey, and is a writer, musician, and teacher.

PICTURE CREDITS

Art Directors & TRIP Photo Library: 6, 11, 27, 28, 32, 34 (bottom), 35, 45, 68, 83, 87
Camera Press: 12, 17, 56, 74
Downtown MoneyPoint: 90 (both)
Alain Evrard: 47
Getty Images/HultonArchive: 13, 14, 16, 39, 57, 58, 59, 63, 73, 75, 76, 77, 78, 79, 80, 81, 82, 84, 85
The Hutchison Library: 3 (center), 5, 20, 66, 72
Iqbal Academy of Pakistan: 54 (both), 55
John R. Jones: 91
Junoon/Ather Shehzad: 60
Earl and Nazima Kowall: 62
Lonely Planet Images: 8, 26, 51
NewsPix: 36
Christine Osborne Pictures: 1, 2, 10, 19, 34 (top), 38, 43, 52, 64, 89
Pakistan High Commission, Singapore: 15 (top)
Pakistan National Council of the Arts: 30 (both), 31 (top)
Peter Sanders Photography: 69
Topham Picturepoint: 3 (top), 7, 9 (both), 15 (center), 15 (bottom), 18, 21, 23, 25, 29, 37, 40, 41, 46, 48, 49, 70, 71
UNAIDS Pakistan and the United Nations Information Centre in Pakistan: 61
Nik Wheeler: cover, 3 (bottom), 4, 22, 31 (bottom), 33, 42, 44, 53, 65, 67
Alison Wright: 24, 50

Digital Scanning by Superskill Graphics Pte Ltd

Written by
JAMEEL HAQUE

Edited by
KATHARINE BROWN

Edited in the U.S. by
PATRICIA LANTIER

Designed by
GEOSLYN LIM

Picture research by
SUSAN JANE MANUEL

First published in North America in 2002 by
Gareth Stevens Publishing
A World Almanac Education Group Company
330 West Olive Street, Suite 100
Milwaukee, Wisconsin 53212 USA

Please visit our web site at
www.garethstevens.com
For a free color catalog describing
Gareth Stevens Publishing's list of high-quality
books and multimedia programs, call 1-800-542-2595
or fax your request to (414) 332-3567.

All rights reserved. No parts of this book may be reproduced or utilized in any form or by any means electronic or mechanical, including photocopying, recording, or by an information storage and retrieval system, without permission from the copyright owner.

© **TIMES MEDIA PRIVATE LIMITED 2002**
Originated and designed by
Times Editions
An imprint of Times Media Private Limited
A member of the Times Publishing Group
Times Centre, 1 New Industrial Road
Singapore 536196
http://www.timesone.co...sg/te

Library of Congress Cataloging-in-Publication Data
Haque, Jameel.
Pakistan / Jameel Haque.
p. cm. — (Countries of the world)
Includes bibliographical references and index.
Summary: Presents information on the geography,
history, government, economy, people, social life and customs,
arts, and relations with North America of Pakistan,
an Islamic country in South Asia.
ISBN 0-8368-2352-4 (lib. bdg.)
1. Pakistan—Juvenile literature. [1. Pakistan.]
I. Title. II. Countries of the world (Milwaukee, Wis.)
DS376.9.H36   2002
954.91—dc21   2001057700

Printed in Malaysia

1 2 3 4 5 6 7 8 9 06 05 04 03 02

Contents

AN OVERVIEW OF PAKISTAN

The Islamic Republic of Pakistan is located in South Asia. Once part of British India, Pakistan was created in 1947 to answer the demands for a separate homeland for Indian Muslims. Initially, the new nation included East Pakistan, which became the independent state of Bangladesh in 1971. Throughout its short history, the country has faced many struggles and obstacles, most notably political instability and economic difficulty.

Pakistan is home to many ethnic groups, whose individual customs and characteristics have added exotic diversity to the country's culture. The country also boasts great natural beauty with towering snow-capped mountains, high plateaus, fertile plains, and sandy deserts.

Opposite: **The streets of Pakistan's major cities, such as Peshawar, are crowded with hawkers selling foods and handicrafts.**

Below: **The Prime Minister's Secretariat Building is located in Islamabad, Pakistan's capital city.**

THE FLAG OF PAKISTAN

The flag of Pakistan is based largely on the flag of the All-India Muslim League, which led the country's independence movement. Shortly before independence in 1947, a vertical white stripe was added to the left-hand side of the flag. Today, Pakistan's flag is dark green with a vertical white stripe. A white crescent and a five-pointed star are in the center of the flag. The dark green represents the nation's Muslim majority. The white stripe symbolizes the country's religious minorities and tolerance of those faiths. The crescent stands for progress, and the star represents light and knowledge.

Geography

Pakistan has an area of 310,400 square miles (803,936 square kilometers). The country borders China to the northeast, India to the east and southeast, Iran to the southwest, and Afghanistan to the northwest and north. The Arabian Sea forms the country's southern border with 650 miles (1,046 kilometers) of coastline.

Mountains

Mountains cover much of northern and northwestern Pakistan. The western ranges of the Himalayas and the Karakoram Range extend across the northern end of the country. The Karakoram Range includes the country's highest peak, K2, at 28,252 feet (8,611 meters). The Hindu Kush Range extends along the Afghan border in the northwestern part of the country.

Indus Plain

The Indus Plain covers an area of about 200,000 square miles (518,000 square km). Extending southward, the plain stretches to the Arabian Sea and contains much of Pakistan's most productive agricultural land.

K2

Pakistan is home to the second-highest mountain in the world. Despite repeated attempts by European and American expeditions to reach its summit, K2 remained unconquered until 1954.

(A Closer Look, page 62)

Below: **Forming one of the highest mountain systems in the world, the Karakoram Range stretches across northern Pakistan.**

Left: The Hindu Kush Range in the northwestern part of the country is the source of many rivers, including tributaries of the Indus River.

THE INDUS RIVER

Flowing for 1,800 miles (2,896 km), the Indus River has played a key role in Pakistan's geography, history, and economy.
(A Closer Look, page 52)

The province of Punjab is in the northern part of this area. Here, the flat lowland is drained by the Indus River and its five lower tributaries. The flatlands between rivers are called *doabs* (doo-WABS) and are densely settled and intensively farmed. As a result, this part of the plain is home to most of the country's population and many of its major urban areas, including Islamabad, the capital city.

The province of Sindh lies in the southern part of the Indus Plain. Much narrower than the plain to the north, Sindh has an average width of about 100 miles (160 km). This area occupies both sides of the Indus River as the river meanders toward the Arabian Sea. Apart from the fertile belt of land along the banks of the river, most of the land is unfit for agricultural use. The eastern part of this region also includes part of the Thar Desert.

KARACHI

Pakistan's commercial center and largest city, Karachi is a sprawling metropolis of traditional and modern buildings, bazaars, and hi-tech electronics shops.
(A Closer Look, page 64)

Balochistan Plateau

Made up of rugged hills, upland plateaus, and mountains, the Balochistan Plateau occupies the southwestern and much of the western parts of the country. The Sulaiman and Kirthar ranges separate this region from the Indus Plain. Its landscape consists mostly of barren rock and sand, and it is the least populated region in Pakistan.

THE KHYBER PASS

Probably the most famous mountain pass in the world, the Khyber Pass links Pakistan and Afghanistan. This pass was one of the traditional trade and invasion routes between Central Asia and the Indian subcontinent. Today, a railroad runs to the Afghan border.

Above: In spring, beautiful apricot blossoms bloom against a backdrop of snow-capped mountains in northwestern Pakistan.

Climate

Pakistan's climate is characterized by extreme variations of temperature. The country's mountain regions have the coolest weather. Summer temperatures in the north and northwest average about 75° Fahrenheit (24° Celsius), while winter temperatures often fall below freezing. In the Balochistan Plateau, summer temperatures are higher at about 80° F (27° C), and winter temperatures drop to less than 40° F (4° C). In the Indus Plain, temperatures range from 90° F to 120° F (32° C to 49° C) in summer and fall to about 55° F (13° C) in winter. The southern coastal region has mild, humid weather for most of the year.

Although Pakistan has a monsoon season between July and September, it is an extremely arid country, with an average of 10 inches (25 centimeters) of rainfall a year. The northern part of the country receives the most rain, ranging from 30 to 35 inches (76 to 89 cm) a year. In contrast, much of the Balochistan Plateau receives less than 5 inches (13 cm) of rain a year. Consequently, the area relies heavily on irrigation from the Indus River. The province of Punjab receives more than 20 inches (51 cm) of rainfall each year.

AIR POLLUTION

One of Pakistan's main environmental concerns is air pollution. According to reports, 90 percent of the pollutants present in the country's air is caused by motor vehicle exhaust emissions. This problem is getting worse as the number of cars on Pakistani roads continues to rise at a staggering rate.

(A Closer Look, page 44)

Plants and Animals

Pakistan's vegetation varies according to elevation. Alpine flora grows in the country's mountainous regions. At lower elevations, forests of spruce, evergreen oak, pine, and a cedar known as the deodar can be found. The mangrove forests of Pakistan's coastal region give way to mulberry and acacia trees and date palms in the sparsely vegetated south.

Animal life abounds in Pakistan. The northern mountains provide homes for numerous types of animals, including brown bears, leopards, black Himalayan bears, and Siberian ibex. Jackals, foxes, wild cats, and a variety of rodents and reptiles make their home throughout the country. Pakistan also has a wide variety of birds of prey, such as imperial eagles, saker falcons, ospreys, and migratory goshawks. Water birds, such as mallards, shovelers, spoonbills, geese, and wood ducks, live in the marshy Manchhar Lake in Sindh.

National parks and wildlife sanctuaries have been set up, especially in the northern and southern parts of the country, to protect Pakistan's valuable wildlife. The two largest national parks are Hingol and Kirthar national parks. Both parks are places of tremendous beauty and are populated with rare species of animals, including striped hyenas and desert wolves.

THE SNOW LEOPARD

A member of the cat family, the rare snow leopard (*above*) lives in the steep terrain of northern Pakistan.
(*A Closer Look, page 70*)

Left: **Making its home in the mountainous regions of northern Pakistan, the Siberian ibex has enormous, back-curving horns that can measure up to 55 inches (140 cm) in males. The animal is remarkably surefooted and is known for its agility in leaping across rocky ridges.**

9

History

Archaeological evidence suggests that the area now known as Pakistan has been occupied for over eight thousand years. By 2,500 B.C., the Indus Valley civilization had emerged in the Indus Valley region. Around 1,500 B.C., a nomadic group called the Aryans moved into the area from Central Asia, bringing an early form of Hinduism with them. In time, they settled across almost all of India (including present-day Pakistan and Bangladesh).

Kingdoms and Empires

The Persians conquered the land up to the Indus River in the 500s B.C. In 327 B.C., Alexander the Great crossed into Punjab and established several Greek settlements there. Between c. 321 and 185 B.C., the area was part of the Mauryan Empire. With the decline of the empire, invaders fought for territories in the north, while regional monarchies gained power in the south. By about A.D. 320, the Gupta Dynasty had established its rule over the region. Toward the end of the 600s, the area was ruled by regional kingdoms that battled each other for control of territories.

THE INDUS VALLEY CIVILIZATION

Flourishing for almost one thousand years, the Indus Valley civilization is believed to be one of the world's first great civilizations. During its existence, well-planned cities, such as Mohenjo-Daro (*below*), and towns were developed, with extensive water supply systems, sewage facilities, and centralized granaries. The cause of the civilization's decline by 1,700 B.C. is still unknown.

Left: This Mughal painting shows Emperor Akbar (*left*), often referred to as Akbar the Great, passing the Mughal crown to his son and heir, Prince Salim, later known as Jahangir (*right*).

The Arrival of Islam

Arab Muslims sailed across the Arabian Sea and invaded Sindh in the seventh and eighth centuries, bringing the religion of Islam with them. Between 1001 and 1027, Afghan sultan Mahmud of Ghazna repeatedly raided northern India and established in Punjab the easternmost part of his large but short-lived empire. In 1206, most of what is now Pakistan became part of the Delhi Sultanate, a Muslim territory that included northern India. The Delhi Sultanate lasted until 1526.

The Mughal Empire

The Mughal Empire was established in 1526 by Turk Zahir-ud-Din Muhammad Babur, a descendant of Genghis Khan. Babur's grandson, Akbar, expanded the empire's territorial boundaries considerably. Music, literature, art, and architecture reached new heights under Mughal rule, and religious tolerance was encouraged. The empire continued to extend its territories and consolidate its power until the end of Aurangzeb's reign at the beginning of the eighteenth century. By then, Aurangzeb's costly military campaigns and growing religious intolerance had begun to undermine the stability of the empire. The disintegration of Mughal authority in the eighteenth century ended the long period during which Muslim rulers had held influence over much of the subcontinent.

DELHI SULTANATE

Established in 1206, the Delhi Sultanate was ruled by five successive dynasties: Slave, Khalji, Tughluq, Sayyid, and Lodi. Faced with internal conflicts, the Slave dynasty ended in 1290. Under the Khalji dynasty (1290–1320), the sultanate's control continued to extend over the subcontinent. Losing their power, the Khaljis were succeeded by the Tughluq dynasty (1320–1413). The power of the sultanate extended even further under the Tughluqs and was recognized far into southern India. By 1351, however, southern India had regained its independence, and much of the north was in rebellion. Following a period of internal strife, the Mongol conqueror Timur invaded India and destroyed Delhi. Under the Sayyid (c. 1414–1451) and Lodi (1451–1526) dynasties, the power of the Delhi Sultanate was greatly reduced.

From British India to Partition

After the Mughal Empire began to break up, the East India Company gained control over much of India. Following the Great Revolt that started in 1857, the British government took over these territories, which were now known as British India, in 1858.

By the end of the nineteenth century, the British had improved infrastructure and introduced their education system into India. Western-educated Hindu Indians soon outnumbered Muslim Indians who continued to attend their own schools. Resentment, however, toward the British grew as the population began to demand greater self-government.

The emergence of independence movements in the early 1900s coincided with increased social, economic, and political differences between the Hindu and Muslim communities. Under the leadership of Mohammed Ali Jinnah, the Muslim League, which had been established in 1906 to represent Indian Muslims, demanded the partition, or division, of British India along religious lines in 1940. By 1947, negotiations between Hindu and Muslim politicians had failed, and the Indian Independence Act of 1947 divided the subcontinent into Pakistan and India.

Above: **Mohammed Ali Jinnah (***third from right***), Viceroy of India Lord Louis Mountbatten (***fourth from right***), and Indian nationalist Jawaharlal Nehru (***sixth from right***), among others, attended a conference in New Delhi (now in present-day India) on June 7, 1947, to discuss the partition of British India.**

MOHAMMED ALI JINNAH

Mohammed Ali Jinnah was the driving force behind the movement for Pakistani independence. Today, he is widely regarded as the father of modern Pakistan.
(A Closer Look, page 58)

A Nation Is Born

Pakistan gained its independence on August 14, 1947. The new nation came into existence in two parts: West Pakistan (now Pakistan) and East Pakistan (now Bangladesh). The first years of independence were turbulent as the government struggled to overcome serious economic and social problems. The death of Jinnah, the first governor general, in 1948 and the assassination of Liaquat Ali Khan, the country's first prime minister, in 1951 were major setbacks in the country's development. Throughout the late 1950s and 1960s, military leaders controlled the government.

Following independence, tensions between West and East Pakistan escalated. Many East Pakistanis resented West Pakistani control over the nation's government and economy, and they began to demand greater autonomy from the West. Following the success of the Awami League (the major political force in East Pakistan) in the general election of 1970 and subsequent failed negotiations with the West's Pakistan People's Party (PPP), civil unrest in the East soon erupted into civil war. War broke out between Pakistan and India when Indian troops invaded East Pakistan in December 1971. The Pakistani army soon surrendered, and East Pakistan became the independent state of Bangladesh on December 16, 1971.

THE AFTERMATH OF PARTITION

Immediately after partition, an estimated one million people were killed in the riots that followed between Hindus and Muslims. In addition, both nations experienced a mass movement of people who now found themselves on the "wrong" side of new international boundaries.

Below: Onlookers cheer Sikh soldiers from East Pakistan's 9th Armoured Brigade during the war for independence against West Pakistan in 1971.

Pakistan Today

After the breakup of Pakistan, Zulfikar Ali Bhutto became president of former West Pakistan. Allegations of Bhutto rigging the 1977 elections led to violent demonstrations and demands by the opposition for a new election. Consequently, Bhutto declared martial law. He was ousted from office in July 1977 by General Mohammad Zia ul-Haq, the country's chief of staff of the army. Zia, in turn, imposed martial law, which lasted until 1985. During his rule, Zia introduced Islamization measures, including the establishment of Shari'a courts to exercise Islamic law.

Following the death of Zia in 1988, Benazir Bhutto, Zulfikar's daughter and leader of the PPP, became prime minister after elections. She was ousted from power twenty months later and succeeded by Nawaz Sharif. A subsequent power struggle between President Ghulam Ishaq Khan and Prime Minister Sharif ensued, and both were forced to resign in 1993. Bhutto was once again named prime minister. Domestic unrest between rival political, religious, and ethnic groups plagued the country in the mid-1990s. In 1996, Bhutto's government was dismissed, and Nawaz Sharif was reelected prime minister. By the end of the 1990s, Sharif faced increasing political and military opposition and a deteriorating economy. In October 1999, General Pervez Musharraf led a coup d'état that returned Pakistan to military rule for the fourth time in the country's short history.

JAMMU AND KASHMIR: A DIVIDED REGION

The region of Jammu and Kashmir has been the center of a dispute between Pakistan and India since partition in 1947. The Kashmir issue is complex and arouses strong emotions on both sides of the border.

(A Closer Look, page 56)

FOREIGN POLICY

From 1979, Pakistan's foreign policy was dominated by the Soviet invasion of Afghanistan. By 1984, around three million Afghan refugees were living along Pakistan's border with Afghanistan. The presence of these refugees prompted ethnic and civil disturbances. When an Afghan peace agreement was reached in April 1988, attention turned to India. By the early 1990s, tension between the two countries had intensified, particularly over the issue of Jammu and Kashmir, and both nations were continuing to pursue nuclear weapons programs.

Left: This Pakistani soldier is standing guard at a checkpoint outside the Punjab Assembly building in Lahore following the bloodless coup of October 1999.

Benazir Bhutto (1953–)

Born in Karachi, Benazir Bhutto is the daughter of Zulfikar Ali Bhutto, the country's prime minister from 1971 to 1977. Bhutto and her mother assumed the leadership of the PPP when her father was imprisoned in 1977 and subsequently executed. After years of detention and living in exile, Bhutto returned to Pakistan in 1986 to head the PPP. When she was named prime minister in 1988, Bhutto became the first woman to head an Islamic country. Although she was ousted from office on corruption charges in 1990, she came back to power in 1993. Bhutto was again removed from power amid allegations of corruption and mismanagement in 1996. Two years later, she and her husband were convicted of corruption. The Pakistani Supreme Court ordered a retrial, which has yet to take place.

Benazir Bhutto

Liaquat Ali Khan (1895–1951)

The son of a landowner, Liaquat Ali Khan entered politics in 1923. He began working closely with Mohammed Ali Jinnah after joining the Muslim League. Liaquat soon gained the respect of the Muslim community for his role in the struggle to bring about an independent homeland for the Muslims of British India. When Pakistan was established in 1947, Liaquat became the country's first prime minister. As prime minister, he laid down the foundations of the country's domestic and foreign policies. He was assassinated in 1951.

Liaquat Ali Khan

Imran Ahmed Khan Niazi (1952 –)

Known as the Lion of Lahore, Imran Ahmed Khan Niazi is regarded as one of the best all-around cricketers to have come out of Pakistan. Khan became the captain of Pakistan's cricket team in 1982. He retired briefly in 1988 before returning to the game in the same year. Khan became a national hero when he captained the country's cricket team to victory in the 1991/92 World Cup. At the height of his cricketing career, he was considered the fastest bowler in the world. After retiring in 1992, Khan entered politics and formed his own political party called Pakistan Tehrik-e-Insaaf in 1996. He has also set up the Shaukat Kahanam Memorial Hospital, which treats people suffering from cancer.

Imran Ahmed Khan Niazi

Government and the Economy

Pakistan's system of government is in a state of flux. As of October 12, 1999, the country's constitution has been suspended and Parliament dissolved following a military takeover by General Pervez Musharraf.

Prior to the military coup, the country was a federal republic whose government consisted of legislative, executive, and judicial branches. The bicameral Parliament, or two-part legislative body, consisted of the National Assembly and the Senate. The National Assembly was made up of 217 members, 10 of which represented non-Muslim candidates, elected directly by Pakistani voters. Members of the National Assembly served five-year terms. The Senate was made up of 87 members who were elected indirectly by the provincial assemblies to serve six-year terms.

The president was the country's head of state. Serving a five-year term, the president was elected by the National Assembly, the Senate, and the four provincial assemblies. The prime minister was elected by the National Assembly and was usually the leader of the majority party or the leader of a majority coalition.

Left: **General Pervez Musharraf, who was the Chief of Army Staff and Chairman of the Joint Chiefs of Staff Committee, became the country's chief executive following the coup that removed Prime Minister Nawaz Sharif from office in October 1999. Although Musharraf has promised to reform the electoral process; create viable, elected local governments; and respect the rule of law and fundamental human rights, little progress toward these milestones has been seen to date.**

THE JUDICIARY

The Supreme Court in Islamabad (*left*) is Pakistan's highest court, and the justices are named by the president. The judicial system in each of the nation's provinces is headed by a high court, the judges of which are also named by the president. District and session courts deal with civil and criminal cases, respectively, while the country's lowest courts consist of village courts and magistrates. The country also has a federal Shari'a Court, which administers Islamic law. In January 2000, all judges were required to take an oath of loyalty to Musharraf's regime.

On October 12, 1999, General Musharraf became the country's chief executive and assumed the role of head of the government. He then appointed a National Security Council consisting of eight members to act as Pakistan's supreme governing body. Musharraf appointed himself president of Pakistan on June 20, 2001, while remaining head of the army. The Supreme Court validated the coup in May 2000 but set a deadline that a general election must be held by October 2002.

Local Government

Pakistan is divided into four provinces. In addition to these provinces, the country has eleven federally administered tribal areas, the Islamabad Capital Territory, and tribal areas administered by provincial governments.

Under the 1973 constitution, each province had popularly elected provincial assemblies, a governor elected by the president, and a chief minister in whom executive power was vested. Each province was divided administratively into divisions that were headed by commissioners. These divisions were further subdivided into districts. Under the military regime of General Musharraf, these structures of local government have been modified. As the provincial legislatures have been suspended, provincial governors report directly to the chief executive.

POLITICAL PARTIES

Although General Musharraf has dissolved Parliament, political parties have been allowed to continue their activities. National political parties include the Pakistan Muslim League (PML) and the PPP. The Awami National Party (ANP), the Mutahida Qaumi Movement (MQM), and the Jamaat-i-Islami (JI) are among the parties that have a strong regional, ethnic, or religious base.

Economy

Since independence, Pakistan's economy has been slowed down by the fast-growing population, high military spending, often unstable political conditions, and mounting foreign debts. Economic problems intensified in the 1990s when sanctions were imposed by foreign nations to protest the country's nuclear weapons program. Many of the sanctions imposed by the United States and Canada were lifted at the end of 2001, clearing the way for urgently required economic assistance.

Agriculture dominates the economy and accounts for 44 percent of the workforce. Only about 25 percent of Pakistan's total land area, however, is under cultivation. Most of the cultivated area is located in Punjab, where both flatlands and usable water are more plentiful than elsewhere in the country. The greatest impact on agriculture has come from the numerous irrigation schemes carried out over the years. Farming production, however, remains limited by primitive methods, and mechanization is uncommon. Pakistan has achieved self-sufficiency in wheat farming. Animals also play an important

Above: **These fishermen unload their day's catch at Karachi's fishing harbor. Although underdeveloped, the country's fishing resources are extensive; the sea surrounding the coasts of Balochistan and Sindh is rich in salmon, anchovies, mackerel, and shrimp.**

role in Pakistan's agricultural economy, and cattle, sheep, goats, water buffalo, and poultry are raised in great numbers.

Seventeen percent of Pakistan's workforce is employed in the manufacturing industry. Cotton textile production is the most important of the country's industries. Other important industries include food processing, construction materials, beverages, and paper products.

Although more than twenty types of minerals have been found in the country, the exploration of Pakistan's mineral wealth is incomplete. Coal mining is one of the country's oldest industries. The quality of the coal, however, is poor, and imports are necessary to meet demand. Petroleum production has increased since the 1980s following the discovery of reserves in Sindh and Punjab provinces. Pakistan also has huge reserves of natural gas located in eastern Balochistan. Other minerals include bauxite, copper, iron ore, rock salt, and sulfur.

Most of the country's power needs are met by oil, which is mainly imported, and natural gas; the remainder is met by hydroelectricity and nuclear power. Despite increases in energy production, Pakistan experiences chronic electricity shortages due predominantly to rapid demand growth.

IRRIGATION

As rainfall is scarce throughout most of the country, irrigation waters are essential for most farming. Millions of acres (hectares) of farmland are irrigated with water from the Indus River and its tributaries. The main means of irrigation are canals that carry river waters. The country has also built six river dams, several hundred miles (km) of new canals that link old canal systems with new sources of river water, and two new dams with large reservoirs. Although this canal irrigation is vital to the existence of Pakistan's agricultural sector, it has ruined millions of acres (ha) of productive farmland due to salinity and waterlogging. The government has set up a salinity-control and reclamation program, but the problem still remains a serious one.

Left: These men and women are threshing rice in the province of Sindh. About two-thirds of Pakistanis are dependent on the land for their main source of livelihood. Apart from wheat, other major agricultural products include cotton, rice, corn, barley, and sugarcane.

People and Lifestyle

Pakistan's population encompasses a range of distinct ethnic groups, each with its own language, culture, and traditions. As a result, the country's people tend to identify themselves first with their communities and then with their nation. Pakistanis can be divided into five main ethnic groups: Punjabis, Sindhis, Pashtuns (also called Pathans), Baloch, and *muhajirs* (moo-HAH-jeerz).

The Punjabis inhabit the province of Punjab and are the most numerous and politically influential group in the country. Making up an estimated two-thirds of the population, Punjabis are divided into castes, the largest of which are the Rajputs and the Jats. As the fertile flatlands of the Indus Plain are located in this area, most Punjabis are employed in the agricultural sector.

Sindhis come from the province of Sindh in the southern part of the country. They are ethnically mixed due to the diverse peoples who settled in the area over the centuries, including those of Arab, Persian, and Turkish origin. Today, the Sindhi population is concentrated in the province's cities and the irrigated plains. Karachi, the country's largest city, is located in this region.

Below: **These young girls attend an all-girls Islamic school in the province of Sindh.**

Left: These men in the northern part of Punjab are taking time out to chat about their families and discuss current affairs. In Pakistani society, the elderly are generally well respected.

The Pashtuns predominate northwestern Pakistan. Most Pashtuns make their home in North-West Frontier, while the remainder live in northern Balochistan. Descended from ancient Aryans and subsequent invaders, Pashtuns are traditionally pastoral nomads with a strong tribal organization. Today, Pashtuns work in agriculture, business, and trade.

The Baloch live in the western province of Balochistan. A seminomadic tribal people, the Baloch are divided into twelve major groups that trace their roots to peoples who originally lived in Syria and settled in their present homeland between the fifth and seventh centuries. They engage in seasonal farming and raising animals.

Native speakers of Urdu, the muhajirs are Muslim refugees, or descendants of refugees, who arrived in Pakistan at the time of partition from India. Interested in commerce, most muhajirs live in the country's large cities, such as Karachi, Islamabad, Hyderabad, and Rawalpindi.

The country is also home to many smaller ethnic groups that still follow their traditional ways of life. Nomadic communities live in the northwestern mountainous region, while others make their home in the Thar Desert. The mountains of the north are home to several groups, including the Hunzakuts and the Dards.

PUKHTUNWALI

Pukhtunwali (PUHK-tuhn-wah-lee) is the Pashtun way of life. The system revolves around a code of honor. Hospitality is extremely important to the Pashtun, and food, drink, and shelter are available to all who seek it. Other codes include maintaining pride and displaying bravery. Pashtuns must also avenge any insult made against themselves, their families, or their tribe. Some feuds can run from generation to generation. Pashtuns also rely on their tribal councils to resolve disputes and make decisions.

HUNZA: A MOUNTAIN KINGDOM

Famous for the breathtaking beauty of its landscape, Hunza is regarded by many as paradise on Earth. It is also allegedly home to the world's healthiest and longest-living people.
(A Closer Look, page 50)

Left: **This extended family in Lahore is enjoying a day out in the family's horse-drawn cart. In Pakistan, the family is the backbone of society, and relatives often gather to share meals and celebrate important occasions, such as the birth of a child and weddings.**

Family Life

The Pakistani family unit is strongly male-oriented, and the eldest male is the dominant figure of the household. Pakistani families tend to be large, and several generations often live under the same roof. Most Pakistanis are very close to their family members and rely on them during times of emotional or financial difficulty.

Most Pakistanis do not choose their spouses. Parents still arrange most marriages. The best match is considered between first cousins because the union strengthens family ties. Pakistani women become members of their husbands' families when they marry. Traditionally, men are responsible for overseeing the agricultural or business activities of the family, while the women run the household, prepare meals, and raise the children.

The majority of Pakistan's urban population lives in the country's major cities. Many urban, well-to-do homes are built

WOMEN IN PAKISTAN

Although Pakistan was the first Islamic state to have a female prime minister, most Pakistani women are struggling to improve their status within society.

(A Closer Look, page 72)

around a central courtyard. The courtyard is used as a garden, an area for children to play, and a place to hold special events, such as weddings. Most city dwellers, however, live in small houses in old, crowded neighborhoods. In recent years, the rapid increase in urbanization, together with the rising population, has added to the housing shortage in urban areas. Today, approximately 25 percent of people in large cities live in shantytowns.

Although Pakistan's cities are highly populated, most Pakistanis are rural, living in villages scattered from the high mountain valleys in the north to the desert areas in the southeast. Villages consist of clusters of houses that are usually made of unbaked mud bricks and roofed with straw. Houses usually have walled courtyards where people sleep in the open in summer and where animals are tied up. The style of rural houses, construction materials, and furnishings varies according to region.

Urban-Rural Divide

Standards of living vary considerably throughout the country. The prosperous urban elite live in large, air-conditioned houses with the latest modern conveniences, while most of the rural poor still lack access to basic infrastructure, such as running water, electricity, and clean drinking water.

HEALTH

Despite improvements in the nation's health standards since independence, many Pakistanis continue to face major health hazards. Leading causes of death include malaria; childhood diseases, such as whooping cough and measles; typhoid; and respiratory infections. Inadequate sewage disposal, lack of safe drinking water, and malnutrition all contribute to health problems.

Left: This mother poses with her children in front of their home in North-West Frontier.

23

Education

Despite the government's objective of providing free and universal education through the tenth year of formal schooling for both boys and girls, the education system in Pakistan is poor. Pakistan faces a huge shortage of schools, particularly in the most remote parts of the country. Schools also suffer from extreme shortages of teaching materials, ranging from textbooks to chalk, and trained teachers.

The Pakistani education system consists of five stages — elementary school, middle school, high school, intermediate college, and university. Pakistani elementary school spans five years and is aimed at children between the ages of five and ten.

Pakistani middle school consists of a three-year course for children aged ten to thirteen. After two years of high school, students take the Secondary School Certificate or Matriculation Examination. Students may then study for a further two years at an intermediate college. At the end of the second year, students take the examinations for the Intermediate Certificate or Higher Secondary School Certificate. Students must obtain the Intermediate Certificate if they want to attend a university.

LITERACY RATE IN PAKISTAN

Only 42.7 percent of Pakistanis over the age of fifteen are literate. The literacy rate in urban areas tends to be higher than in rural areas. Children born in remote, underdeveloped areas of the country have few opportunities to obtain an education and, therefore, less chance of breaking the cycle of poverty.

Below: These schoolchildren attend a school for both boys and girls in Gulmit in the northern region of Pakistan. Coeducation, however, is not common in most parts of the country.

Founded in 1882, Punjab University is the country's oldest university. Other major universities are in Islamabad, Karachi, and Peshawar. Pakistan's first university for women, the Fatima Jinnah Women's University, was opened in 1998 and is located in Rawalpindi.

The Gender Gap in Education

While the enrollment rate in elementary schools is high for boys, the number of girls attending elementary school is much lower. Pakistan also trails behind its South Asian neighbors in the education of girls and women. Traditionally, the education of boys has been more important than the education of girls in Pakistan. Many families rely on their daughters to help in the home. Parents are also concerned about the conditions under which their daughters are taught and the gender of the teachers. In recent years, the government has acknowledged the importance of educating the female population and is attempting to set up more schools with female-only teachers to encourage more parents to send their daughters to school.

Above: **These young boys in the province of Balochistan are attending class in a makeshift classroom set up outdoors. Attendance at school is low in rural areas, where there is little or no access to schools. In addition, many parents need their children's help in the fields.**

Religion

Islam is the official religion of Pakistan, and 97 percent of the population is Muslim. Seventy-seven percent of the country's Muslims belong to the Sunnite branch, while 20 percent are Shi'ite. All Muslims believe in one God, and that Muhammad is His prophet. The differences in belief between Sunni and Shi'ite Muslims arose after the death of Prophet Muhammad and still divide the two branches today. Shi'ites regard Muhammad's direct descendants as the only legitimate leaders of the Islamic world. Sunni Muslims, however, accept other claims to leadership.

The Islamic faith has five principles, known as the Five Pillars of Islam, that every Muslim should follow. The first principle is the declaration of faith a Muslim performs by reciting, "There is no God but Allah and Muhammad is His messenger." The second is to pray to Allah five times a day. The third principle involves donating money to the poor and needy. The fourth principle involves fasting during daylight hours for one month during the Islamic holy month of Ramadan. The fifth principle is for every Muslim to make a pilgrimage to the holy city of Mecca, in Saudi Arabia, once in his or her lifetime.

Below: **These Muslim men are going to pray at Badshahi Mosque in Lahore. Completed in 1674, the mosque, which is made of red sandstone, was built by Mughal emperor Aurangzeb.**

Above: **This Sikh temple, which is known as Dera Baba Nanak Gurdwara, is located in Lahore. The city is home to a small Sikh population.**

Minority groups exist within the country's Shi'ite Muslims. These groups include the Ismailis and the Ashari. The Ismailis recognize the Aga Khan as their leader and have a strong presence in the northern mountain area of the country, while the Ashari is a prominent community in business and commerce.

Sufism

The tradition of Islamic mysticism known as Sufism remains strong in Pakistan. Sufism is an aspect of Islam in which Muslims seek to find the truth of divine love and knowledge through direct personal experience of God. The followers of the various Sufi orders number more than half of the population.

Other Faiths

Three percent of Pakistanis are non-Muslim. They are free to practice their religion, as long as they respect Islam. The leading minority religions are Hinduism and Christianity. The largest concentration of Christians is in the province of Punjab, while most Hindus live in eastern Sindh. Other religious minorities include Sikhs, Parsis, and a small number of Buddhists.

27

Language and Literature

About twenty languages and numerous dialects are spoken throughout Pakistan, reflecting the country's ethnic diversity. The majority of these languages belong to the Aryan branch of the Indo-European language family. Forty-eight percent of the population speaks Punjabi. Other languages include Sindhi; Pashtu, the language of the Pashtuns; and Balochi, one of the two main languages of Balochistan. Brahui, the other main language in Balochistan, is linguistically related to the languages of southern India.

Due to the presence of regional languages and dialects, the government has adopted Urdu as an official language of Pakistan. Urdu was chosen because it was not identified with any regional or ethnic group. Although the language is similar to the Indian language Hindi, Urdu emphasizes words of Persian and Arabic origin and is written from right to left. Despite the government's

Left: Daily newspapers are published in Urdu, English, and a few other languages. The leading Urdu-language daily is *Daily Jang*. Although English language newspapers are read by less than 1 percent of Pakistani people, newspapers such as *Dawn* and *Pakistan Times* are still influential.

Left: **These Muslim boys are learning to read the Koran at a religious school in Karachi.**

MUHAMMAD IQBAL

Not only is Muhammad Iqbal the country's national poet, but he also played a key role in the birth of Pakistan. Iqbal was the first to suggest the formation of a separate independent state for the Muslims of the subcontinent.

(A Closer Look, page 54)

attempt to promote Urdu as a unifying language, it is spoken by only 8 percent of the population. English is the other official language of Pakistan. Although only a small number of people speak English, it is used extensively by people in government, the military, business, and higher education.

Literature

Pakistan has a rich literary tradition, notably in Urdu, which has been used for literary purposes since the sixteenth century. Muhammad Iqbal (1877–1938), who lived before the establishment of Pakistan, is the country's most famous poet. Using the poetical vocabulary of classical Persian-Urdu, Iqbal transformed Urdu poetry into a vitalizing art.

Contemporary Pakistani writers who have won recognition include the Urdu poet Faiz Ahmad Faiz (1911–1984) and the Urdu short story writer Saadat Hasan Manto (1912–1955). Sometimes considered a controversial writer, Faiz's poetry expresses a strong socialist spirit. The works of Saadat Hasan Manto deal with the dark side of life, and his story *Toba Tek Singh* is one of the best pieces of literature written about the human tragedy experienced during the upheaval of the 1947 partition. Since the 1950s, writers have produced poems and stories that deal with pressing social issues. The writings of Ahmad Nadeem Qasimi (1916–) deal mainly with rural life, a topic with which many Pakistanis can relate.

REGIONAL LITERATURE

Each region in Pakistan maintains a rich literary heritage in its own predominant language. Classical poetry in Sindhi dates from the sixteenth century, while modern Sindhi authors produce short stories, historical novels, and biographies. Punjabis have many folk tales, ballads, and epics that have been passed down orally from one generation to the next. Poetry is important in the Pashtu language. The themes of the poems reflect the harsh struggles that the Pashtuns have faced throughout the centuries. Balochi has a rich folk literature of ballads and legends.

Arts

Painting

Painting flourished under the Mughal rulers, and the styles that developed during this period have had a lasting effect on Pakistani art. One of the favorite themes of Mughal paintings was nature; portraits were another. With the decline of the Mughal Empire and its patronage of the arts, British influences gradually became evident as painters began to make more use of depth, shadows, and perspective. Abdur Rahman Chughtai (1897–1975) is acclaimed as the foremost national painter of Pakistan. In his efforts to filter out British influences, he revived the traditional Mughal style of art, and his paintings are regarded as classics.

The advent of modern art arrived in Pakistan in the 1950s. Influential artists of the time included Zubeida Agha (1922–1997) and Shakir Ali (1916–1975), who embraced Western influences. Breaking away from traditional themes, Agha's paintings were abstract in theme. Shakir Ali introduced cubism to Pakistan, and many of his themes borrowed from classical European myths. As his style evolved, he reduced the human form to sharp angles and used red as a dominant color. Many of his paintings feature birds, which he regarded as the symbol of personal freedom. Sadequain

MAGNIFICENT MOSQUES

The Mughals first introduced Islamic architecture to Pakistan and encouraged the mixing of Persian, Indian, and local styles in the construction of mosques. Today, however, a new style of mosque that consists of tentlike structures with slim minarets is superseding imitations of the traditional Mughal forms.
(A Closer Look, page 66)

CENTERS OF ART

At the time of independence, Lahore was the arts center of the country, and the city's Mayo School of Art (now the National College of Arts) and Punjab University's Fine Arts Department were the only recognized art institutions in Pakistan. By the 1950s, Karachi had also joined the mainstream of national art.

Left: These two paintings are based on the poetry of Mirza Asadullah Khan Ghalib (1797–1869) and were painted by Sadequain in 1968.

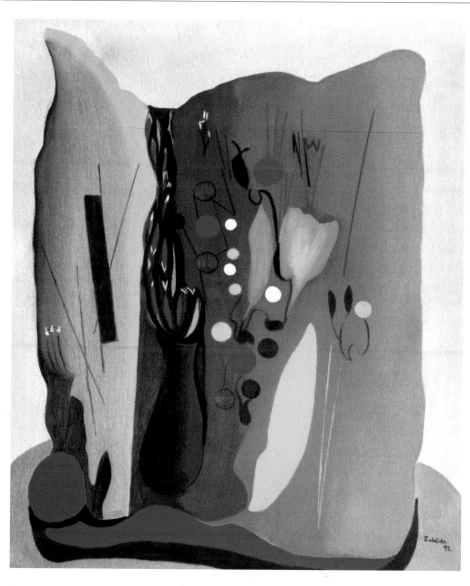

Left: *Blue Vase* was painted by Pakistani artist Zubeida Agha in 1993.

ART ON THE MOVE

From the mountain ranges in the north to the Balochistan Plateau, ornate and colorful vehicles (*below*) loaded with people and goods are seen moving through Pakistan's landscape. Regarded as a modern art form, decorating trucks and buses is popular all over the country. Decorations include landscapes and flowers of the driver's home area; animals, such as lions, which express power, speed, and strength; and machines, such as airplanes and trains, that show admiration for technology. Quotations from the Koran and pictures of Muslim holy places often cover the front part of the vehicle.

(1930–1987) was a popular artist, and much of his work is displayed in public places throughout the country. He first produced sketches and figure paintings and then moved on to calligraphy and murals.

Miniature Art

Miniature painting is a traditional art form that remains popular today. Originating during the Mughal period, this type of painting is highly stylized and requires years of apprenticeship. Painted using fine brushes made of squirrel's tail, the subject matter of these tiny paintings is usually religious or literary, although historical events are sometimes illustrated.

CALLIGRAPHY

Calligraphy, the art of elegant handwriting, has flourished in the area now known as Pakistan for centuries. Calligraphic inscriptions, such as this one, were used in abundance to decorate the beautiful mosques built during the Mughal period. These inscriptions were usually poems or verses from the Koran. Today, calligraphy and calligraphic paintings continue to adorn mosques and buildings, as well as everyday objects, such as plates and vases.

Metalwork

Pakistan is renowned for its highly decorative metalwork. Metalsmiths use damascening to create intricately designed objects, such as trays, goblets, and platters. The most popular pattern is the intertwined flowering vine composed of rosettes and arabesques. Metalworkers also apply enamel to their products to add a color glaze to the metal.

Handicrafts

Every region in Pakistan specializes in local arts and crafts, including embroidered and appliquéd bedspreads and table linen, leather goods, woodwork, lacquerware, and gold and silver jewelry. The handicrafts of Punjab include traditions that date back thousands of years. Today, village potters continue to make clay toys that resemble the figurines recovered from the archaeological sites of the Indus Valley civilization. Sindh is particularly noted for its textiles, embroidery, pottery, and lacquerware. Mirrorwork, the sewing of tiny pieces of mirror onto cloth, is typically Sindhi and decorates the brightly colored clothes of many Sindhi women.

THE ART OF CARPET WEAVING

Famous for its beautiful patterned wool, silk, and cotton carpets, Pakistan's carpet weavers are among the most valued in the world.
(A Closer Look, page 46)

Folk Dances

Pakistan's diverse ethnic groups perform an amazing array of energetic and powerful folk dances. One of the country's most popular dances is *bangra* (BAHNG-rah). Originating from Punjab, young men dressed in brightly colored clothes gather in a circle around a drummer who beats out the rhythm of the dance. Moving around the drummer, slowly at first, then faster as the tempo of the drum quickens, the men dance and sing. Originally performed during the Hindu New Year, the dance is now performed on special occasions, such as weddings. *Khattak* (KHU-tuhk) is a sword dance of the Pashtun that is performed by men in colorful costumes, including elaborate waistcoats. Another folk dance is *kathak* (KUH-tuhk), a north Indian style of classical dance that is distinctly Hindu-Muslim. Performed by both men and women, the dance is characterized by the rhythmic footwork of the dancers who skillfully control ankle bells. The intricate footwork and spectacular, rapid spins are the most interesting features of this style. Kathak was originally a temple dance that the Mughals adapted to a court dance. Although it currently has a limited audience, the dance is making a gradual comeback in Pakistan.

JUNOON

The rock group Junoon is a household name in Pakistan and has millions of adoring young fans.
(A Closer Look, page 60)

MUSICAL TRADITIONS

From the beat of the tabla to the sound of the sitar, traditional Pakistani music boasts a rich heritage.
(A Closer Look, page 68)

Left: **These Sindhi men are performing an enchanting and rhythmic folk dance that is characteristic of the province.**

Leisure and Festivals

Opportunities for leisure and entertainment are limited in many parts of Pakistan, particularly in rural areas. Consequently, most leisure activities revolve around the family. In the evenings, many families enjoy sitting in their courtyards and chatting. Social get-togethers are the major form of entertainment for many of the country's ethnic groups, such as the Pashtun, Punjabi, and Sindhi. Religious holidays are also times when family and friends gather.

Social interaction also occurs at the local mosque. After Friday prayers, many people stay at the mosque to meet with distant relatives and friends to chat and exchange news. Weekly markets also attract large crowds. Popular rural activities among men include cock-fighting, pigeon-racing, and camel-racing.

More forms of entertainment are available in the country's cities. Families often have picnics in public parks or have hours of fun at amusement parks. Larger cities, such as Karachi and Lahore, also provide extra forms of family entertainment, such as camel and horse rides.

Above: **Pakistanis are passionate about films and love going to the movies, such as this one in Karachi. Movies are available in all but the smallest villages, and they are seen as a form of escapism from daily life.**

Left: **These girls are enjoying a camel ride in one of Lahore's public parks.**

Left: **Playing board games is a favorite pastime for many Pakistani children.**

Radio and television are available throughout Pakistan. Television programs include news and current affairs programs, popular quiz programs, dramas highlighting social issues, soap operas, and reruns of old comedy shows from the West. Many well-to-do households also own video recorders, and videotapes can be rented from bazaars.

Children's Games

Pakistani children play local variations of games such as hide-and-seek, marbles, and tag. Another popular game involves a ball and some pebbles. The first player bounces the ball and tries to pick up as many pebbles as possible before catching the ball. When the player misses the ball, the next child takes his or her turn. The child who can pick up the most pebbles and catch the ball is the winner.

Kite flying is also a popular activity throughout the country. To add an extra thrill to their hobby, children coat their kite strings with ground glass to make the strings sharp. They then use the strings to sever their opponents' kite strings in airborne "fights." The children get very excited when a kite string is cut, and they chase the kite until it lands. The child who finds the kite gets to keep it.

Sports

Pakistanis enjoy a wide range of sports and are passionate supporters of their international sports teams. The country has produced prominent athletes, notably in cricket, field hockey, and squash.

The entire country is addicted to the game of cricket, a sport that was introduced into the area that is now Pakistan during the British colonial era. In recent years, the Pakistani national cricket team has regularly defeated the English team, as well as those of other cricketing nations. Some of the world's best cricketers come from Pakistan, including Imran Khan, Wasim Akram, and Mushtaq Ahmed.

Field hockey is also an extremely popular sport. An outdoor game played by two opposing teams of eleven male players, the aim of the game is to score as many goals as possible by hitting a small, hard ball into the opposing team's net. The game is played at local, provincial, and national levels. The country's national field hockey team is one of the best in the world. The team has won the Olympic gold medal three times and the World Cup Field Hockey Championship four times.

Pakistan excels at squash, a game similar to racquetball, and the country has produced many fine squash players, including

CRICKET

Extremely popular in Pakistan, cricket is played with a bat and ball between two teams of eleven players.

(A Closer Look, page 48)

Left: **Pakistan's Atif Bashir (*left*) runs past his Malaysian counterpart during a preliminary match between Pakistan and Malaysia in the men's hockey event during the 2000 Olympic Games held in Sydney, Australia. The teams drew 2–2.**

Left: Jahangir Khan (*left*) plays Jonah Barrington (*right*) in the British Open Championships in 1987. Khan beat Barrington and went on to win the tournament after beating fellow countryman Jansher Khan in the finals. Jahangir Khan became the world's youngest winner of the World Open Championship at the age of seventeen, and he won the prestigious British Open Championships title ten times in a row.

Jahangir Khan and Jansher Khan. Another sport that has always been played in Pakistan is *kabaddi* (kah-buh-DEE). Requiring skill and power, the game is a combination of wrestling and tag.

Polo ranks as a favorite sport in the northern part of the country. A stick-and-ball game, polo is played on horseback by two teams of six players. The object of the game is to strike the ball with a handheld mallet into the opposing team's goal. An alternative form of polo is played in the province of North-West Frontier. In this version, the ball is replaced with the body of a goat, which two opposing teams try to gain control of and drop into the designated scoring area.

Other popular sports include soccer, tennis, badminton, and table tennis. Pakistanis also participate in track and field events.

Women in Sports

Women are underrepresented in the Pakistani sports world. They can perform in front of female-only audiences and are expected to follow Islamic dress codes. Although women do participate in track and field events, play volleyball and cricket, and compete in racquet sports, such as tennis and badminton, they find it a challenge to further their sporting careers.

KABADDI

Kabaddi is played by two teams that aim to gain the higher score by touching or capturing the players of the opposing team. One player, or "raider," enters the opponents' court, chanting "kabaddi kabaddi." He then tries to touch any or all of the opposing players and return to his own court in one breath. Any player that is touched is out. The aim of the opposing team is to stop the raider from returning to his own court until he takes another breath. If the team succeeds, the raider is out. Each team takes turns sending a raider into the opposing court. As this game is inexpensive and can be played almost anywhere, it is very popular among the rural population.

Festivals

Pakistan celebrates many religious festivals. Other festivals honor national heroes or commemorate political events in the nation's recent history.

Religious Festivals

The ninth month of the Muslim calendar is Ramadan, the Muslim month of fasting. During this time, no healthy adult Muslim should eat, drink, or smoke during daylight hours. After a month of fasting, the end of Ramadan is celebrated with the sighting of the new moon, and *Eid ul-Fitr* (EED OOL-fitr) follows. After going to the mosque in the morning to pray, parents give gifts to their children, visit relatives and friends, and entertain guests. *Bakr-Id* (BUK-rah EED), the Feast of the Sacrifice, falls in the last month of the Islamic year. Commemorating Abraham's willingness to sacrifice his only son to God, this festival is celebrated with the sacrifice of goats and sheep, and the distribution of the meat to relatives, friends, and the poor.

URS

Pakistani Muslims have festive days called *urs* (OORS) that honor Sufi saints. These festivals are celebrated at the shrine where the saint is buried and can last several days. Worshipers say prayers and offer money, incense, flowers, sweets, and sometimes a cloth that is used to cover the tomb. The Koran is read, and religious songs are sung throughout the night.

National Holidays

Pakistanis also celebrate a number of national holidays. Pakistan Day on March 23 honors the day in 1940 when the Muslim League passed its resolution demanding an independent state for the Muslims of the subcontinent. Independence Day on August 14 celebrates the country's break with Britain and India and its establishment as an independent nation. The day is marked by celebrations, fireworks, and feasting, and households and businesses throughout the country display the national flag. Commemorating the 1965 Pakistan-India conflict, Defence of Pakistan Day takes place on September 6. On this day, military parades take place throughout the country. The birth- and death-anniversaries of Mohammed Ali Jinnah (December 25 and September 11, respectively) are also celebrated.

Minority Festivals

Pakistan's religious minorities, including Christians, Hindus, and Sikhs, have their own holidays. Christmas, Good Friday, and Easter Sunday are celebrated by the country's Christian community.

Opposite: **Muslims pray at Badshahi Mosque in Lahore on the morning of Eid ul-Fitr.**

Below: **Pakistani soldiers participate in a military parade in Islamabad, the country's capital, to celebrate Pakistan Day on March 23.**

39

Food

Although Pakistani food shares a common heritage with that of neighboring India, a number of factors help distinguish the two cuisines. Pakistani cuisine tends to be less spicy because its dishes are often made with yogurt, which reduces the effect of the hot spices commonly used in cooking. Herbs and spices are also extremely important to Pakistani cuisine. Their use in a wide range of pickles, chutneys, and sauces gives Pakistani cooking much of its distinctive character.

The daily diet for most Pakistanis consists of bread, rice, vegetables, and some type of meat. The most common type of bread is chapati, which is round and flat and resembles a tortilla. When heated, the chapati puffs up and becomes soft. Other popular breads are nan and *paratha* (puh-RAH-tah), which is a chapati fried in butter. Rice also comes in a variety of forms. Apart from plain white rice, there is also *biryani* (bir-YAH-nee) rice, which is cooked in a meat sauce. Favorite vegetable dishes

DIETARY LAWS

Pakistani Muslims have a set of dietary laws that are prescribed by religion. Pork is considered unclean and is not eaten by the Muslim population. In addition, Pakistani Muslims only eat halal meat and do not consume alcoholic beverages.

Left: Herbs and spices, such as red chilies, ginger, garlic, cumin, coriander, and garam masala, play a key role in the preparation of any Pakistani dish.

Left: The imaginative use of spices, herbs, seeds, seasonings, and flavorings helps cooks transform ordinary staples into exotic dishes.

include seasonal vegetables; spiced pulses known as dal; and *sag* (SAHG), or mustard greens. All these vegetable dishes are cooked with garlic, onion, chilies, cloves, black pepper, and ginger. Those who can afford it eat meat or poultry. Goat meat is a favorite.

The Mughal style of cooking is dominant throughout Pakistan and emerged from the royal kitchens of the Mughal emperors of India between the sixteenth and eighteenth centuries. Instead of using the hot spices of regular Indian cuisine, Mughal cooking makes use of a blend of herbs and spices. Mughal food includes a selection of meats and poultry served in sauces or cooked in yogurt; tandoori dishes baked in a hot, clay oven; flat breads; and rice dishes.

Each of the country's provinces has its own specialties. Punjabis are well known for their bread and dals, while Sindhis are known for their seafood dishes. A thick bread baked in an oven that is eaten with cubes of meat, fish, or poultry is a favorite dish among Pashtuns.

Pakistanis love fruits, including mangoes, citrus fruits, pomegranates, guavas, papayas, and berries. Pakistanis also have a sweet tooth and enjoy a wide range of desserts, all of which are delicious and extremely rich.

BEVERAGES

Tea is the most popular drink in Pakistan. It usually comes with milk and plenty of sugar. Spices, such as nutmeg, cinnamon, or cloves, are also sometimes added. Other favorite drinks in Pakistan include *lassi* (LASS-ee), which is made from yogurt, and mango juice.

SWEET DESSERTS

From pastries to slices of fried bread cooked in cream, sweetened in syrup, and topped with nuts and saffron, Pakistani cuisine boasts an amazing array of rich, sweet desserts. Sugary, homemade sweets, which are also considered desserts, are also brought out and shared among family and friends to celebrate happy occasions, such as the birth of a child, a wedding, or a graduation.

A CLOSER LOOK AT PAKISTAN

Pakistan was born through the struggles and perseverance of Mohammed Ali Jinnah, who made the vision of poet Muhammad Iqbal a reality by helping to create a separate state for the Muslims of British India. Since its independence, the country's short history has been marked by war and conflict with neighboring India. Even today, Pakistan is often associated with its ongoing dispute with India over the divided territory of Jammu and Kashmir.

Pakistan boasts fascinating geographical features. Flowing through the length of the country, the Indus River gives life to many areas that would otherwise be barren. The nation's

Opposite: **Worshipers attending Friday noon prayers spill out onto a street in Lahore.**

northern region contains snow-capped mountains, including the formidable K2. This area is also home to the mountain kingdom of Hunza and the majestic, threatened snow leopard.

Pakistanis celebrate their rich cultural heritage in everyday life. They have preserved traditional trades, such as carpet weaving, and play and watch cricket with fervor. In addition, their music embraces the traditional sounds of the tabla and sitar as well as the rock music of Junoon. The country, however, is struggling to overcome the deepening problem of air pollution, which has already begun to affect the health of many city dwellers.

Above: **Ox-drawn carts are a common mode of transportation throughout Pakistan.**

Air Pollution

Pakistan's attempts to improve the living standards of its citizens and the growth of industrialization have meant that economic development has largely taken precedence over environmental issues. Today, one of the most serious concerns facing the Pakistani environment is air pollution. The problem has grown rapidly in recent years and is continuing to do so at an alarming rate.

Air pollution refers to air contamination caused by toxic chemicals or other materials. The leading source of air pollution in Pakistan comes from vehicles, which release major pollutants into the atmosphere. These pollutants include carbon monoxide, carbon dioxide, nitrogen oxides, and hydrocarbons.

Over the past twenty years, the number of vehicles on Pakistani roads has risen at a staggering rate. In 1980, Pakistan had 680,000 cars. By 1998, this number had swelled to 3.8 million. Many of these vehicles burn poor-quality fuel and emit 550 tons (499 metric tonnes) of lead into the atmosphere each year.

CLOSELY RELATED

Air pollution is closely related to water and soil pollution. For example, toxic chemicals, such as sulfur dioxide and nitrogen oxides, can react with water droplets in the air to produce acid rain. Acid rain pollutes lakes and streams and, in high concentrations, can also harm soil fertility.

Left: Although vehicle emissions are the main source of air pollution in Pakistan, factories, such as this one in Karachi, are emitting increasing amounts of toxic pollutants into the atmosphere as the country's industrial sector expands.

Degrading Air Quality

The quality of air in the country's towns and cities is getting worse as a result. Today, the level of air pollution in Pakistan's two largest cities, Karachi and Lahore, is estimated to be twenty times higher than World Health Organization (WHO) standards and is still rising. Islamabad, the country's capital, is continuously smothered by a thick cloud of smog. It has also been estimated that two thousand deaths a year are due to air pollution, and about 6.4 million hospital admissions and 418,000 cases of minor sickness occur every year due to illnesses related to air pollution.

Too Little, Too Late

The government has only recently begun to take action against the degrading air quality in major cities. The Pakistan Environmental Protection Council has formed a committee to look into measures that will reduce pollution in urban areas, while the authorities are investigating the possibility of using alternative fuels for vehicles. Attempts to legislate environmental protection, however, have fallen short, and regulations have not been enforced rigorously enough. It therefore remains to be seen whether the government will place greater importance on environmental protection to curb the country's environmental degradation and protect the health of its citizens.

Opposite: Fumes from traffic clogging the streets of Pakistan's cities, including Peshawar, contribute greatly to the country's air pollution problem. According to the National Conservation Strategy Report (NCSR) released by the government in 1992, the average Pakistani vehicle not only releases 25 times as much carbon dioxide as the average U.S. vehicle but also produces 20 times as many hydrocarbons and more than 3.5 times as many nitrous oxides every 0.6 miles (0.96 km).

The Art of Carpet Weaving

Some of the world's most beautiful carpets come from Pakistan. Made by skilled carpet makers, Pakistani carpets have been used traditionally for sitting, sleeping, and praying. Some carpets dating back hundreds of years record historical events that have taken place in the area now known as Pakistan. Other carpets are appreciated purely for their exquisite designs.

Although the patterns for Pakistani carpets tend to vary from region to region, certain basic designs and motifs predominate, including wavy lines with abstract patterns and geometric shapes. The "elephant foot" design, which resembles diamond-shaped octagons, is probably the most characteristic pattern in Pakistani carpets. Other popular motifs include flowers, fruits, and animals.

Pakistani carpets can contain as many as twenty different colors. Natural dyes, including the indigo plant, bark, and fruits, have traditionally been used to produce the rich, wonderful colors. In recent years, the use of chemical dyes, such as chrome

Opposite: **These carpet sellers in Lahore are admiring the fine workmanship that has gone into making this beautiful carpet. Today, carpet weaving is a flourishing industry in Lahore and Karachi, with 95 percent of output going into the export market.**

Left: **Most of the carpets produced in Pakistan are made in individual homes, which may contain several looms. Some carpet makers, such as these two weavers in the province of Punjab, even weave outside in side streets.**

dye, has increased, but vegetable dyes still remain popular. Pakistani carpets are made of various combinations of wool, cotton, and silk. In carpets, the precision in design relies on the density of the knots. The number of knots per square inch (square cm) is a useful indication of the carpet's quality and durability. The finest Pakistani carpets can have up to 2,500 knots per square inch (6.45 square centimeters).

A Step Back in Time

Carpet weaving in Pakistan began long before the country became an independent nation. Mughal emperor Akbar the Great set up the first workshops for the production of carpets in present-day Lahore in the sixteenth century. As Persian weavers supervised many of these workshops, carpet designs were heavily influenced by those of Persia. In the years that followed, weaving in the region developed at an impressive pace. After the partition of British India in 1947, many carpet weavers migrated from India and settled around the large weaving centers located in and around the cities of Lahore and Karachi.

CHILDREN AND CARPET-MAKING

Millions of Pakistani children work in carpet-making factories all over the country. Valued for their small hands and agile fingers, which are perfect for tying the fine knots used to create the patterns, children work for up to twelve hours a day and are paid very low salaries. Many children work to help earn money to support their families. Following increasing international criticism of the practice, the Pakistani carpet-making industry has agreed to phase out the employment of children under the age of fourteen.

Cricket

Cricket is an ancient and complex game and has a huge following in Pakistan. The origins of cricket are unknown, but a version of the game is believed to have been played in England by the thirteenth century. The sport was introduced to India and present-day Pakistan by British settlers during the eighteenth century. Today, cricket is played throughout Pakistan at local, provincial, and national levels. In addition, the country often competes against England, Australia, New Zealand, India, South Africa, and the West Indies in international, or "Test," matches.

A Complicated Game

Cricket is played by two teams of eleven players each on a large field, known as a ground. The aim of the game is for one side to score more runs than the other team.

The main action takes place at the center of the ground on a pitch, which is 66 feet (20 m) long and 10 feet (3 m) wide. Centered at either end of the pitch is a 9-inch (23-cm)-wide

Opposite: **Members of Pakistan's national cricket team celebrate the dismissal of England's Graham Thorpe on the final day of the 1st Cornhill Test held in London, England, in 1996. Although cricket is a tough and fast sport, it still retains the elegance that once inspired the British to declare it a gentlemanly sport. Today, Pakistan has some of the world's best cricket players and one of the world's best international teams.**

EQUIPMENT AND DRESS

The cricket bat can be a maximum of 38 inches (96.5 cm) in length. The handle is made of cane, while the rest is made of willow. The cricket ball has a hand-stitched red leather cover, and its interior consists of cork wound with string. The ball weighs between 5.5 and 5.75 ounces (156 and 163 grams). A batsman (*left*) wears protective equipment, such as pads, or leg guards, and batting gloves. Some batsmen also choose to wear protective helmets. The wicketkeeper also wears pads and other protective equipment.

The striker scores a run if he hits the ball far enough so that both batsmen can run to exchange places. If the ball crosses the boundary of the field on the ground, four runs are scored automatically. If the ball clears the boundary in the air, six runs are scored. An outstanding turn at batting may result in more than one hundred runs, which is known as a century. The striker does not have to run after he has hit the ball nor does it matter if he misses the ball. If an even number of runs is scored, the striker faces the next ball. If an odd number is scored, the nonstriker will receive the ball as the bowler will be at the opposite wicket.

DISMISSAL

The striker or a batsman can be dismissed ten different ways, including bowled, caught, stumped, hit wicket, and run out. A striker is out "bowled" when the bowler breaks the wicket; "caught" when a fielder catches the ball before it touches the ground; "stumped" if the batsman is outside his safe ground, and the wicketkeeper dislodges the bails of the wicket; or "hit wicket" when a batsman dislodges a bail from his own wicket unintentionally. Either batsman can be "run out" if his wicket is broken while he is out of his safe ground.

wicket consisting of three thin stumps, or poles, placed upright in the ground. On top of the stumps are two bails, or crosspieces, balanced in grooves in the stumps.

The batting team places one batsman at each wicket. The first batsman is known as the striker, and his partner is called the nonstriker. As a pair, the batsmen try to make as many runs as possible without being put out, or dismissed.

The nonbatting team consists of a bowler, a wicketkeeper, and nine fielders. The bowler and wicketkeeper face each other at opposite wickets. The fielders position themselves roughly in two rings around the striker. The bowler bowls the ball to the batsman from the opposite wicket in a series of six, sometimes eight, balls, called overs. When an over is completed, the wicketkeeper moves to the other wicket, and a different bowler begins bowling to the batsman's partner at the opposing wicket. The bowler tries to retire the batsman by "breaking the wicket," or knocking down the bails of the batsman's wicket.

Each side has two innnings that are usually taken alternatively. An innings is completed when ten batsmen have been dismissed. The remaining batsman, who no longer has a partner, is declared "not out."

Hunza: A Mountain Kingdom

With majestic, snow-capped mountains, vast glaciers, and beautiful orchards, Hunza is well known for its picturesque beauty, as well as the longevity of its people. Located in the northern tip of Pakistan, Hunza lies in the Pakistan-controlled part of Jammu and Kashmir and is near the borders of China and Afghanistan.

For hundreds of years, Hunza was an isolated state ruled by a *mir* (MEER), or prince. By the end of the nineteenth century, however, the kingdom had become a princely state that was protected by the government of British India. Pakistan gained control of the area in 1949. The mir was allowed to rule over local matters until 1974, when Pakistan took over complete control. For more than 960 years, this small kingdom was ruled by the same family, known as the mirs of Hunza.

THE BALTIT FORT

For over nine hundred years, the Baltit Fort served as the residence of the mirs of Hunza. According to local legends, the fort was built by three hundred laborers as part of the dowry of a princess who married the then reigning mir. The present mir donated the fort to the Baltit Heritage Trust, which has restored and renovated the fort into a museum.

Left: Hunzakut women lay out apricots and peaches to dry in the sun. These fruits are an integral part of the Hunzakuts' diet.

MORE THAN JUST WATER!

The well-publicized life span of the Hunzakuts has created the belief that the water from Hunza holds magical powers that allow the drinker to lead a long and healthy life. Hunza water, also called glacial milk because of its whitish appearance, comes from the melting ice of the area's surrounding glaciers. Research has shown that the water from this area contains different minerals and a lower surface tension than most other kinds of drinking water. Having a lower surface tension means the water can be absorbed more easily into the body to hydrate the body's cells. The fact that Hunza water has a lower surface tension is one of the main reasons why this glacial milk has a reputation of being a real fountain of youth.

Opposite: The Hunzakuts live in simple houses made of stone. The tranquility of the area has stirred the imagination of many people, and it is believed that this valley and its inhabitants inspired the classic fable of Shangri-La described in the novel *Lost Horizons* by James Hilton.

A Long Life

The people of Hunza are called Hunzakuts. The majority of the population is Muslim and speaks mainly Burushaski, although Urdu and English are also understood. Most Hunzakuts are farmers who grow crops such as barley, grapes, plums, and wheat. Women produce traditional handicrafts and beautiful handwoven woolen cloth called *pattu* (puh-TOO). This colorful, intricate form of embroidery is used to make ladies' caps, gowns, and waistcoats.

Hunzakuts are world famous for their longevity as most of the population lives over the age of ninety. The Hunzakuts believe that their stress-free lifestyle, mineral-rich mountain water, and simple diet contribute to their long life. This low-fat diet consists of fruits, such as apricots and peaches; grains; nuts; and vegetables.

Legends of a Kingdom

According to one legend, the mirs of Hunza are descended directly from Alexander the Great. Another popular legend has it that the Hunzakuts are descended from three soldiers from the army of Alexander the Great who settled in the area that is now Hunza in the 300s B.C. with their Persian wives.

The Indus River

With a length of about 1,800 miles (2,896 km), the Indus River is the chief river of Pakistan. The Indus is also the source of one of the largest irrigation systems in the world, and its life-giving waters sustain an important agricultural economy.

The River's Course

The Indus River rises in southwestern Tibet and flows northwest between the Himalaya and Karakoram ranges. The river plunges through some of the world's deepest gorges and scenic valleys as it twists among the mountains. The river crosses the western border of Jammu and Kashmir and then turns south and southwest to enter Pakistan. Flowing as a rapid mountain stream, the river eventually enters Punjab, where it receives waters from its five main tributaries. After receiving these waters, the Indus becomes much wider and flows at a slow speed, depositing large quantities of silt along its course. The river then breaks into distributaries that drain into the Arabian Sea.

River of Life

Irrigation from the waters of the Indus River has supported the basis for successful agriculture for thousands of years. Pakistan's

THE INDUS WATERS TREATY

Although Pakistan and India signed the Indus Waters Treaty in 1960, which stated that the waters of the Indus were to be shared, the use of the river and its tributaries continues to be a source of conflict between the two nations.

Left: **Many fishermen make their living from the waters of the Indus River. The river is moderately rich in fish, and the country's leading fishing centers are located in the province of Sindh.**

Above: **The Indus River enters the plains of Punjab northeast of Attock.**

most densely populated region is the irrigated plains of Punjab province. This province is also the country's main agricultural area; wheat, corn, rice, millet, dates, and fruits are the chief crops. The Indus also provides irrigation for millions of acres (ha) of arid land in the province of Sindh.

The Indus and its tributaries are used extensively for the generation of hydroelectric power. The Tarbela Dam, located northwest of Rawalpindi, is the world's largest earth-filled dam and has the capacity to generate 3,478 megawatts of electricity.

Although the river brings great benefits to the regions it irrigates, these areas are prone to flooding during the rainy monsoon season. In 1992, flooding in the northern area of the Indus was the worst it had been for almost a century, killing over two thousand people and damaging crops, roads, and bridges.

An Endangered Species

The Indus River is home to the Indus River dolphin, one of the rarest mammals in the world. The dolphin originally inhabited the entire Indus River system, but the construction of dams and barrages along the river has split the population into small groups, degraded habitat, and prevented migration. In an attempt to save the Indus River dolphin, the government of Sindh province has declared the mammal a legally protected species and has established the Indus River Dolphin Reserve.

Muhammad Iqbal

Muhammad Iqbal is Pakistan's most famous poet. Also a philosopher, Iqbal is credited with being the first to project the concept of a separate Muslim state in the Indian subcontinent.

Iqbal was born on November 9, 1877, in Sialkot, India (now in Pakistan), into a family of small merchants. After attending Government College in Lahore, Iqbal studied philosophy at Cambridge University and qualified as a barrister in London before receiving a doctorate from the University of Munich. He then returned to Lahore to practice law. Iqbal, however, gained a national reputation for his Persian- and Urdu-language poetry.

Above: **Blending philosophy into his poetry, Muhammad Iqbal is regarded as the greatest Urdu poet of the twentieth century. Iqbal was knighted in 1922, and Iqbal Day is celebrated every year by Pakistanis.**

The Power of Poetry

Iqbal's early poetry supported Indian nationalism. Upon his return from Europe, however, his poems and essays promoted the revival of Islam. He originally wrote in Urdu but began to write in Persian as well so that his writings would appeal to the entire Muslim world. His first Persian poem was *Asrar-e khudi* (1915), or *The Secrets of the Self*. Its sequel, *Rumuz-e bikhudi*, or *The Mysteries of Selflessness*, was published in 1918.

Left: **Muhammad Iqbal (*center*) poses for a photograph with two colleagues from the Muslim League in 1929.**

Left: **Muhammad Iqbal (*second from left*) attends a conference with members of the Muslim League in the early 1930s. Iqbal became a key figure in the Muslim League after his historic speech delivered at the 1930 annual session of the Muslim League, in which he suggested the idea of an independent homeland for Indian Muslims.**

Through his poetry, Iqbal urged a regeneration of Islam through the love of God and the active development of the self. He also encouraged Muslims to embrace the ideals of brotherhood, justice, and service. In a society where it was customary for people to memorize and recite poetry, his works became well known, even among the lesser educated and illiterate classes. Iqbal's masterpiece is widely considered to be *Javid-nameh*, or *The Song of Eternity*. Written in 1932, the poem is similar in theme to Dante's *Divine Comedy* because it traces the poet's ascent through all realms of thought and experience, guided by the thirteenth-century mystic Jalal ad-Din ar-Rumi.

By the late 1920s, Iqbal had become actively involved with the Muslim League, an organization that protected the rights of Indian Muslims. In his presidential address to the Muslim League in 1930, Iqbal made a famous speech in which he suggested that the Muslims of northwestern India should demand a separate nation for themselves. This proposal was the first step toward the eventual formation of Pakistan.

The Death of a Poet

Iqbal died in Lahore on April 21, 1938, two years before the Muslim League voted for the idea of Pakistan. Although he died before his dream could be realized, Iqbal played a key role in creating the idea of a separate homeland for Indian Muslims.

Jammu and Kashmir: A Divided Region

Located in the northern part of the Indian subcontinent, Jammu and Kashmir (commonly known as Kashmir) is currently divided between three neighboring countries: Pakistan, India, and China. The territory lies at the heart of tensions between Pakistan and India, and its northern border is also disputed by China.

The History

The conflict began in 1947 when the Indian subcontinent was split along religious lines. Under the partition plan in the Indian Independence Act of 1947, Kashmir was free to accede to either Pakistan or India. Maharaja Hari Singh, the ruler of Kashmir at that time, was Hindu while most of his subjects were Muslim. Although the maharaja wanted Kashmir to remain independent, he eventually ceded the land to India on October 26, 1947.

Three Wars

Pakistan did not accept the accession as legal and argued that the region should have become part of Pakistan because most Kashmiris were Muslim. Indian and Pakistani forces fought their

THE DIVIDED AREAS

The Indian-controlled portion of the territory has been organized into the state of Jammu and Kashmir. At present, China occupies the northeastern part of Ladakh, which originally formed part of the land claimed by India. Pakistan administers the northwestern portion of the territory, which is known as Azad Kashmir and the Northern Areas.

A PARADISE LOST

Once known as the "Switzerland of the East," Kashmir (*left*) is surrounded by some of the highest mountains in the world and has deep lakes and lush forests. The land is home to many game animals, including ibex, stags, and bears. Most of the population is employed in the agricultural sector, and silk and carpet weaving are major industries. Until 1989, about 500,000 Indians and foreigners visited Kashmir each year. Today, the region is considered too dangerous to visit.

Left: Pakistani president General Pervez Musharraf (*left*) shakes hands with Indian prime minister Atal Behari Vajpayee (*right*) during the Agra Summit held in July 2001. During the three-day summit, Musharraf and Vajpayee discussed bilateral relations and their nuclear weapons programs. Talks, however, ended without an agreement, with the long-running dispute over Kashmir seen as the main reason for the deadlock.

first war over Kashmir from 1947 to 1948. After the United Nations (U.N.) intervened, a cease-fire agreement between the two nations was concluded in January 1949. Under the agreement, a Line of Control (LOC) was drawn up, with 65 percent of the territory under Indian control and the remaining 37 percent with Pakistan. This partition was regarded as a temporary measure but still exists today. Subsequent efforts by the U.N. to hold a plebiscite have been unsuccessful.

Heavy fighting broke out between the two sides in 1965 and again in 1971. Following the Simla Agreement of 1972, both countries vowed to resolve the Kashmir issue through peaceful means and to respect the LOC that resulted from the cease-fire of December 1971.

A Continuing Stalemate

The Kashmir problem is far from over as violence in the war-torn region continues to escalate. With the emergence of pro-Pakistan and pro-independence guerrillas since 1989 and increasingly frequent clashes between Indian and Pakistani troops, an estimated thirty thousand soldiers and civilians were killed during the 1990s. Today, about eighty thousand Indian and Pakistani troops currently face each other along the LOC.

THE THIRD PLAYER

After China annexed Tibet in 1950, the Chinese built a road through the northeastern part of Kashmir to link Tibet with the Chinese mainland. The existence of this road led to the Sino-Indian war in October 1962. Emerging victorious from the war, China has since occupied the northeastern part of Ladakh region.

Mohammed Ali Jinnah

Through tireless effort and complete devotion, Mohammed Ali Jinnah helped bring about the creation of an independent nation for the Muslim population of British India in 1947. Since then, he has been considered the father of Pakistan.

Born in Karachi (then in India) on December 25, 1876, Jinnah first entered politics in 1906 when he participated in the Calcutta session of the Indian National Congress, a political organization that was working for Indian autonomy from British rule. He began his long and illustrious parliamentary career four years later when he was elected to the Imperial Legislative Council. Believing that Hindu-Muslim religious conflicts could be overcome, Jinnah's ultimate goal was to create a united India.

Above: **Mohammed Ali Jinnah received legal training at Lincoln's Bar in London, England, and became a lawyer in Bombay (now Mumbai), India, before turning to politics in 1906.**

The Ambassador of Hindu-Muslim Unity

In 1916, Jinnah was hailed as the ambassador of Hindu-Muslim unity due to his key role in bringing about the Lucknow Pact. The pact was a united demand by the Indian National Congress and the All-India Muslim League for the transfer of greater political power from the British. One important right to emerge from the pact was the principle of separate electorates for Indian Muslims.

By 1920, Mohandas K. Ghandi had emerged as a powerful political figure. His noncooperation movement, which was a mass campaign to boycott all aspects of British rule in India, led Jinnah to resign from both the League and the Congress in 1920. Nevertheless, Jinnah continued to believe in the possibility of Hindu-Muslim unity. He attended the Round Table Conferences in London (1930–1932), which discussed India's political future. Frustrated with the rejection of his compromise proposals, Jinnah moved to England until 1935.

Jinnah was persuaded to return to British India and reorganize the Muslim League (formerly the All-India Muslim League) for the elections to be held under the Government of India Act of 1935. Jinnah's hope of cooperation between the League and the Congress ended in 1937 when, in the elections, the Congress gained an absolute majority in six provinces and rejected Jinnah's proposal to form coalition provincial governments. As a result, tension between Hindu and Muslim Indians grew rapidly.

THE EMERGENCE OF THE ALL-INDIA MUSLIM LEAGUE

With increased demands for greater independence from British rule at the beginning of the twentieth century, the general feeling among Indian Muslims was that they should retain a separate identity rather than be part of an Indian nation that would be mainly Hindu. As a result, the All-India Muslim League was founded in 1906 to protect the interests of Indian Muslims. Jinnah joined the league seven years later.

Founder of Pakistan

Although Jinnah had supported the idea of a united India for most of his political career, he soon acknowledged that a separate Muslim nation was the only way Muslim interests could be protected. Under Jinnah's leadership, the Muslim League adopted a resolution to create a separate Muslim state called Pakistan in March 1940. Capturing the imagination of Indian Muslims, the creation of the new country would mean the preservation of their religious and cultural traditions and more economic opportunities for the Muslim middle classes. The Congress rejected the resolution, and the British wanted the Indian subcontinent to remain politically unified. Jinnah's skill and tenacity, however, made the dream of Muslim Indians a reality when both the Congress and the British government finally accepted the partitioning of British India and the creation of independent Pakistan in 1947.

Jinnah became the first governor general of Pakistan on August 14, 1947. Although he died shortly after the establishment of the new state on September 11, 1948, Jinnah was and still is revered by Pakistanis as the Quaid-i-Azam, or Great Leader.

Left: **Mohammed Ali Jinnah (***second from left***), the first governor general of Pakistan, salutes during a military parade in Karachi on August 17, 1947.**

Junoon

Dubbed by many as one of the biggest bands in the world, Junoon is the most popular band in Pakistan. The name of the group is taken from the Urdu word *junoon* (juh-NOON) meaning "passion," and it is the band's passion for its music that has stirred the emotions of so many young Pakistanis.

Consisting of Salman Ahmad, Ali Azmat, and Brian O'Connell, Junoon plays an eclectic brand of music that mixes the mystical Urdu poetry of Sufi saints with Punjabi and Sindhi folk music and rock 'n' roll of the West. Junoon first made an impact on the Pakistani music scene in 1996 when its single "Jazba-e-Junoon" became Pakistan's anthem for the cricket World Cup. Since then, the band has steadily increased in popularity.

The band members have never shied away from controversy, and they have faced heavy criticism from successive governments. Their music and videos were banned by the governments of Benazir Bhutto and Nawaz Sharif, and the group was prohibited from performing at large-scale concerts. Despite these setbacks, Junoon's popularity continued to skyrocket. All restrictions against the group were lifted after the military government of General Musharraf came to power in 1999.

CONTROVERSIAL

Success and controversy have always gone hand-in-hand for rock band Junoon. Song lyrics criticizing Pakistani politics led to the ban of their music during the government of Benazir Bhutto. The government of Nawaz Sharif kept the ban in place after the band declined to write a charity song aimed to help the government raise money to pay off some of its debts to the International Monetary Fund (IMF). The group angered the government further when Salman Ahmad made comments suggesting that Pakistan and India should work to improve social conditions within their countries rather than compete in a nuclear arms race.

Left: No other band in Pakistan is as popular as Brian O'Connell (*left*), Ali Azmat (*center*), and Salman Ahmad (*right*), who together form the rock band Junoon.

Left: **Junoon's Salman Ahmad is the national spokesman for UNAIDS Pakistan. He was also selected to appear on a poster that promoted the 2001 "I care... do you?" World AIDS Campaign. According to UNAIDS Pakistan, Ahmad's background as a medical doctor and his extreme popularity among the young people of Pakistan have placed him in a unique position to raise awareness about HIV/AIDS. In June 2001, Ahmad attended a special session of the U.N. General Assembly on HIV/AIDS to further highlight his support in the fight against the disease.**

More Than Just a Band

Not only does Junoon's music entertain millions of fans, it has also done much to bring pressing social issues to the attention of its young audience. As a band, the members have spoken out against nuclear weapons and urged for unity around the world. For their efforts, they have won accolades from international organizations and received an award from the United Nations Educational, Scientific, and Cultural Organization (UNESCO) for their achievements toward peace in South Asia, particularly between Pakistan and India.

Most recently, guitarist and songwriter Salman Ahmad was appointed by the U.N. to be their national spokesperson for the 2001 campaign against HIV/AIDS in Pakistan. By selecting Ahmad, the U.N. hopes to make Pakistanis aware of Acquired Immune Deficiency Syndrome (AIDS) and the human immuno-deficiency virus (HIV) that leads to AIDS.

K2

Reaching an elevation of 28,252 feet (8,611 m), K2 is the world's second-highest mountain, after Mount Everest. The mountain, which forms part of the Karakoram Range, straddles the border between China and Jammu and Kashmir. Pakistan currently controls the area in which K2 lies.

Regarded by many mountaineers as the ultimate climb, K2 was discovered and measured by Colonel T. G. Montgomerie of the Survey of India in 1856. Following its discovery, the mountain was named K2 because it was the second peak to be measured in the Karakoram Range. In 1861, the peak was unofficially named Mount Godwin-Austen, after the peak's first surveyor, Colonel H. H. Godwin Austen.

Failed Attempts

Below: Formidable K2 rises above the surrounding mountains that form part of the Karakoram Range. Apart from the name K2, the mountain is also known locally as Chogori.

The first attempt to climb K2 was made by an Anglo-Swiss expedition in 1902. The team tried to reach the summit via the mountain's northeastern ridge but only managed to ascend to 18,600 feet (5,670 m). An Italian expedition followed seven years later. Led by Luigi Amedeo, Duke d'Abruzzi, the expedition

THE PERILS OF K2

Many factors make K2 one of the most challenging mountains to climb on Earth. The natural formation of the mountain, which has slopes of 45° or more, has often been described as a cone of ice and limestone, and climbers need about 8,202 feet (2,500 m) of rope to climb the south side routes and up to 16,405 feet (5,000 m) of rope for the north ridge route. Unpredictable weather patterns also make climbing a hazard because sudden and blinding blizzards can descend without warning on unsuspecting mountaineers, who are then forced to take shelter (left).

reached about 20,000 feet (6,906 m) via the southeastern ridge (later renamed the Abruzzi Ridge) before the team conceded defeat. In 1938 and 1939, two American expeditions ascended K2 via the Abruzzi Ridge, reaching about 26,000 feet (7,925 m) and 27,500 feet (8,382 m), respectively. American Charles Houston, who had led the unsuccessful 1938 expedition, failed again to reach the summit in 1953. K2, however, did not remain unconquerable for much longer.

Success at Last!

In 1954, an Italian expedition led by Ardito Desio began its ascent of K2. After battling severe weather conditions and overcoming various setbacks, including the death of one of the guides, two team members, Achille Compagnoni and Lino Lacedelli, eventually reached the summit at 6 p.m. on July 31. Wanting the whole team to be credited with the success, Desio did not allow the names of the two climbers to be made public until the team had returned to Italy.

PAKISTANI AT THE PEAK

As part of a Japan-Pakistan joint expedition, Ashraf Aman was the first Pakistani to reach the summit of K2 in 1977.

Karachi

The largest city and principal seaport in Pakistan, Karachi boasts an eclectic mix of modern skyscrapers, nineteenth-century Victorian-Gothic buildings, tree-lined boulevards, and dusty alleys. The city is located on the coast of the Arabian Sea and is the capital of Sindh.

From Humble Beginnings

Kalachi-jo-Goth, as Karachi was then known, began as a small fishing village. By the time the settlement was captured by the British in 1839, it had developed into a trading center due to its strategic position along the coast of the Arabian Sea. Annexed in 1842, Karachi continued to develop. With the opening of the Suez Canal, which connected the Mediterranean and Red seas, in 1869, Karachi's importance as a seaport grew. By 1914, it had become the largest grain exporting port of the British Empire.

When Pakistan became an independent nation in 1947, Karachi became the capital and principal port of the country,

Below: **Markets offering an endless variety of goods can be found throughout the sprawling city of Karachi.**

64

Left: **The mausoleum of Quaid-i-Azam, the founding father of Pakistan, is a prominent landmark in Karachi. Located in the heart of the city, the mausoleum is built entirely of white marble and stands on a raised platform.**

as well as an industrial, commercial, and administrative center. The city remained the seat of government until 1959, when Rawalpindi served as a provisional capital until Islamabad became the country's permanent capital city in 1967.

A City of Wonders

Modern Karachi delights visitors with its mix of old and modern architecture. Popular attractions include the mausoleum of Quaid-i-Azam, or Mohammed Ali Jinnah; the National Museum; the Sindh Legislative Assembly buildings; and the city's numerous bazaars. The National Museum houses an amazing collection of artifacts from the early Indus Valley civilization, as well as pieces of Greco-Buddhist art of Gandhara (a region of ancient India that is now in northwestern Pakistan). Empress Market is probably the most well-known bazaar in Karachi. First opened in 1889, the market houses hundreds of shops and stalls that sell handicrafts, such as copper and brass oryx, inlaid woodwork, lacquerwork, printed and embroidered cloth, leather products, and jewelry, as well as meat, fruits, and vegetables. The city's parks and surrounding beaches are ideal for those who want to get away from the hustle and bustle of city life.

AN INDUSTRIAL AND FINANCIAL HUB

Karachi is an important center for industry and finance. Products manufactured in the city's industrial districts include wool and cotton textiles, household consumer goods, clothing, and machine tools. Karachi also handles all of the country's seaborne trade, as well as that of Afghanistan, its landlocked neighbor. The city is also an important banking center and has a stock exchange.

Magnificent Mosques

Mosques play a pivotal role in the lives of most Pakistanis and are a central feature of every city, town, and village. Considered by many as the nation's greatest works of art, some of the country's most impressive mosques date back to the Mughal period, when Islamic architecture and art flourished to new heights. Throughout the centuries, Mughal designs continued to be imitated. A new style of mosque, however, has emerged in recent years that is moving away from traditional Mughal forms.

Wazir Khan Mosque

Wazir Khan Mosque is one of the most beautiful mosques in Pakistan. Made of brick, the mosque is faced with mosaics of brightly colored glazed tiles depicting Mughal floral motifs, arabesques, and calligraphic panels. The interior of the mosque is decorated with rich and elaborate frescoes and enamel mosaics. In addition, its floor is artistically paved with bricks that form intricate geometrical patterns.

UNIVERSAL FEATURES

Despite variations in design and size, all mosques have features in common. A mosque has four minarets, or towers, one of which is used by the muezzin to call Muslims to prayer. Prayers are said in a prayer hall by a prayer leader who faces Mecca, Islam's most sacred city. A fountain is located outside the main entrance of the mosque, usually in a courtyard, to allow worshipers to wash before entering the mosque to pray.

Above: **The Shah Faisal Mosque in Islamabad resembles an eight-sided Bedouin tent surrounded by four towering minarets that can be seen for miles (km) around.**

The mosque itself is divided into five compartments, each opening into a large courtyard and covered by a dome. The central of these, the main prayer hall, is marked by a framed portal that protrudes from the facade. Octagonal minarets standing at each corner of the courtyard dominate the mosque.

Shah Faisal Mosque

Shah Faisal Mosque in Islamabad is a perfect example of the new style of mosque that has emerged in Pakistan. Its tentlike structure and slim minarets represent more modest and graceful forms of Muslim architecture. The outside walls are faced with marble, and the interior is decorated with blue mosaics. The prayer hall has been designed to accommodate ten thousand worshipers, and the covered porticoes and verandas can hold an additional twenty-four thousand. The mosque's main courtyard has space for another forty thousand worshipers. Considered to be the world's largest mosque, Shah Faisal Mosque was designed by a Turkish architect and financed largely by donations from Saudi Arabia. Shah Faisal Mosque is not only a place of worship, it also houses an Islamic research center, a library, and a museum.

Opposite: **Located in Lahore, Wazir Khan Mosque was built around 1634. The mosque is accessed through a gate leading into a forecourt that functions as a bazaar. A flight of stairs leads onto the raised platform on which the mosque is built.**

Musical Traditions

The musical traditions of Pakistan are rich and diverse and have blended styles and rhythms that originated from many other countries, including Afghanistan and India.

Popular Instruments

A wide variety of exciting instruments are used to play traditional Pakistani music. The tabla is a pair of small drums that consists of a small right-hand drum and a larger left-hand drum. The right-hand drum is usually made of wood, while the left-hand drum is made of iron, copper, aluminum, steel, or clay. The large black spot on each of the playing surfaces creates the bell-like timbre characteristic of this instrument. The sitar is a large, guitarlike instrument. It has a long, broad, fretted neck and a small, pear-shaped body. Due to its six to seven main strings and nine to thirteen sympathetic strings, the sitar can create a large variety of sounds. Originally from Afghanistan, the *rabab* (ruh-BAHB) is similar to a banjo. It is played by plucking the strings and creates short, fast sounds. The *sarangi* (suh-rung-GEE) is a small stringed instrument that is carved from a single piece of wood. Most sarangis have three playing strings that are played with a

Left: **These musicians from Peshawar are playing the sitar (*left*) and the tabla (*right*). These two instruments usually form part of any ensemble that performs Pakistani traditional music.**

KING OF QAWWALI

Regarded as one of the world's greatest singers of Sufi devotional music known as qawwali, Nusrat Fateh Ali Khan (*left*) enjoyed a huge following that spanned generations. Born in 1948 into one of Pakistan's most revered families of qawwals, Khan became famous for his hypnotic live performances where he sang cross-legged on stage. In the years before his death in 1997, Khan also gained a following in the West, notably after his performance on the soundtrack for the Hollywood movie *Dead Man Walking* (1995).

bow. The harmonium, or *baja* (BAH-jah), was originally brought to the Indian subcontinent by the British in the nineteenth century. It resembles an organ and has hand-pumped bellows. The musician plays the keyboard with the right hand, while the left hand pumps the bellows. The *bansari* (BAHN-sree) is a bamboo or reed flute used traditionally in folk music.

Sounds and Rhythms

A distinct form of Pakistani traditional music is *qawwali* (kah-VAH-lee), a type of Islamic religious music. Unlike classical performances that revolve around one person, a group usually performs a qawwali. Within the group is one main singer, or *qawwal* (kah-VAHL), and a number of supporting vocalists. Common musical instruments that accompany a qawwali include the tabla, harmonium, sarangi, and rabab. The audience also participates in the performance and claps to help create the rhythm. The pace of the music gradually increases until a state of extreme excitement is produced.

Today, many new forms of music are emerging in Pakistan. Some of these styles are extensions of traditional forms, while others combine traditional and Western music to create new and exciting sounds and rhythms.

The Snow Leopard

Making its home in Central Asia, the elegant and agile snow leopard is among the most secretive of large carnivores. Shy by nature, this member of the cat family is rarely seen in the wild because its fur enables it to blend in well with its surroundings. Nevertheless, this majestic animal has been endangered since the 1960s.

A Solitary Animal

The snow leopard makes its home in the steep, rocky terrain of the northern, mountainous areas of Pakistan. Weighing up to 165 pounds (75 kilograms), the animal has gray fur with dark rosettes and spots; this fur, which is long and thick, helps keep it warm. A female snow leopard usually has two to three cubs that hunt with their mother through their first winter. Once a snow leopard reaches adulthood, however, it shuns companionship and lives alone. The animal builds its den in places with good views, such as cliff ledges, so that it can look out for enemies. The snow leopard is an opportunistic predator. Its most common prey include wild sheep and goats, but it also eats marmots, hares, and domestic sheep and goats.

Opposite: **This snow leopard is eating its catch of the day. An excellent long jumper, the snow leopard usually stalks its prey, then makes a final lunge, sometimes from above and from as far away as 50 feet (15 m). Because the snow leopard lives in regions where prey is sparse, it tends to range over a wide area to get enough food, moving to a new place each day and migrating to different altitudes to follow prey.**

Left: **Each snow leopard has a home range, an area in which it hunts, drinks, rests, and sleeps. The animal is well adapted to live in its mountainous habitat. Its large forepaws, short forelimbs, and powerful chest muscles enable it to leap quickly from rock to rock, while it uses its long, bushy tail to help it balance as it jumps. Pakistan is currently home to about three hundred snow leopards.**

Endangered!

The continued destruction of the animal's habitat and the spread of human settlement in its hunting ranges have led to a reduction in the number of wild animals that form the snow leopard's usual prey. As a result, the snow leopard has turned its attention increasingly toward domestic sheep and goats. Farmers desperate to protect their livestock often shoot or poison this unwanted predator. Illegal poaching is another major threat facing the snow leopard. For years, the snow leopard has been regarded as a highly prized catch due to its valuable fur. Recent years have also seen an increase in demand for snow leopard bones in Eastern medicine due to the decline in availability of tiger bones.

What Is Being Done?

The Pakistani government and international organizations, such as the International Snow Leopard Trust, acknowledge the need to protect the endangered snow leopard. They aim to set up programs designed to raise the awareness of local communities about this rare animal. Buffer zones have also been set up to establish extra distance between the snow leopard's natural habitat and nearby towns and villages.

AN ONGOING BATTLE

Today, the trade in snow leopard skins and bones is prohibited under the Convention on International Trade in Endangered Species (CITES). Nevertheless, a thriving black market still exists because collectors are willing to pay up to U.S. $3,000 to own a rare snow leopard pelt.

Women in Pakistan

The role of women in Pakistan's society is extremely complex. While some of the country's leading politicians, journalists, and teachers are women, attempts to increase educational and healthcare provisions to the country's female population continue to be hampered by traditional attitudes toward the role of women.

Traditionally, the woman's place in Pakistani society is low and is restricted to the performance of domestic chores and being a dutiful wife and mother. This long-held view has meant that few girls attend school, and the literacy rate of the female population stands at 29 percent. The main reason for this inferior status is the concept of purdah, or the seclusion of women. A woman in purdah spends most of her life within her home. On the rare occasions that she does leave her home, she must wear a *burqa* (BOOR-kah), a long garment that covers her from head to toe, and be accompanied by a male relative. Purdah is observed by wealthy peasant and landowner houssholds and in urban families where it is not necessary for the women to work. Poor rural women, especially in Punjab and Sindh provinces, do not observe purdah because they are expected to work on the farms.

Below: **These Pakistani women are visiting Khyber bazaar in the city of Peshawar. One woman (*left*) is wearing a burqa, while the other women wear thin veils around their head and shoulders.**

Left (from left to right): President Musharraf; First Lady Sehba Musharraf; Attiya Inayatullah, member of the National Security Council; and Zubaida Jalal, Minister for Education, Women's Development, Social Welfare, and Special Education, attended the National Convention of Women in Islamabad on March 8, 2000.

CONFLICT OF OPINIONS

The idea of women working in Pakistan is controversial. While the government has pledged to boost the number of women in the workforce, many families still do not want female relatives to work. In addition, the country's Islamic groups have expressed their concern about increasing job opportunities for women. Some believe that women should continue to stay at home with their families, while others state that if women have to work, they should not mix with men.

FIRST WOMEN BANK

Opened in 1989 by the government of Benazir Bhutto, First Women Bank was established to provide banking facilities to women, as well as help them set up their own businesses. To date, the bank has financed over fourteen thousand female entrepreneurs.

Change is happening gradually. In the country's metropolitan cities, more and more women from the higher classes have stopped observing purdah. These women have begun to pursue academic studies and have gained entry into the workforce.

Women's organizations, such as the All Pakistan Women's Association, work hard to fight for the rights of women. Over the years, these organizations have faced many challenges and have been involved in numerous programs aimed at increasing female literacy, gaining access to employment opportunities, and changing the perception of women's roles and status. The government has also made some attempts to change the position of women in society. At the fourth World Conference on Women held in Beijing in 1995, Pakistan approved a course of action to improve conditions for its female population and signed the Convention on the Elimination of All Forms of Discrimination Against Women.

Although some progress has been made, the majority of Pakistani women still have a long way to go before they achieve some form of liberation from their traditional roles in society.

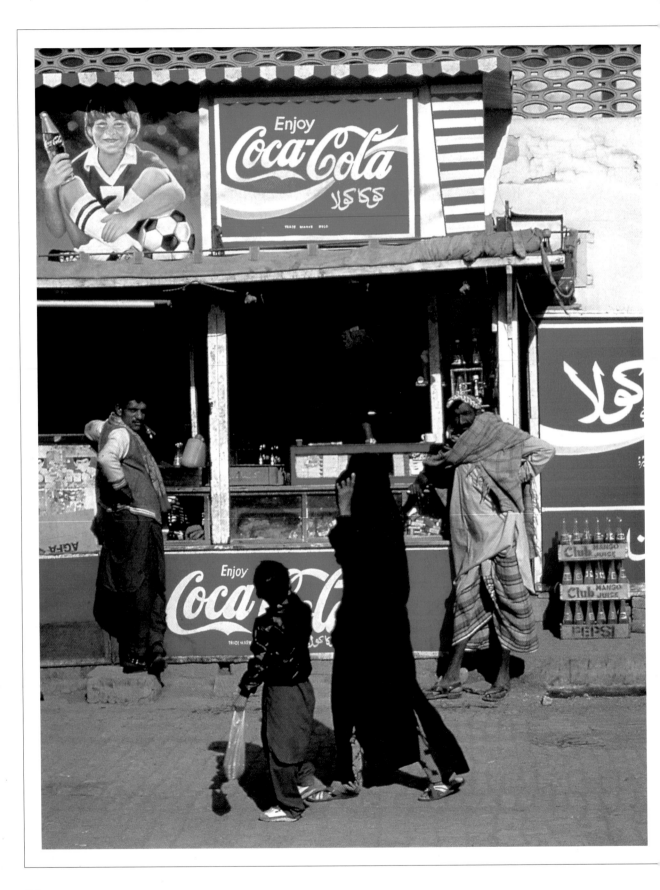

RELATIONS WITH NORTH AMERICA

Relations with North America began after Pakistan gained its independence from the British in 1947. Ties between Pakistan and Canada have, on the whole, been warm. The friendship between Pakistan and the United States, however, has been strained at times. Relations between Pakistan, Canada, and the United States deteriorated in 1998, following nuclear tests carried out by Pakistan. Both the United States and Canada joined the international community in condemning the tests and imposed sanctions as a form of protest. The U.S. and Canadian

Opposite: **Popular North American products, such as Coca-Cola, are available throughout Pakistan.**

governments also denounced the military coup of 1999, and the United States imposed further sanctions. The sanctions imposed by the United States and Canada have had a devastating effect on Pakistan and its economy.

Today, the relationship between the three countries has entered a new stage following President Musharraf's agreement to cooperate with the U.S.-led coalition against global terrorism. Both the U.S. and Canadian governments, however, continue to stress the urgent need for Pakistan to return toward the path of democracy and economic reform.

Above: **Pakistani schoolchildren wave Pakistani and American flags during a rally in Islamabad to celebrate Pakistan Solidarity Day on September 27, 2001. This was one of several rallies held throughout the country to support President Musharraf's agreement to join the U.S.-led coalition against terrorism.**

Historical Ties

Ties between Pakistan and North America were established in 1947 after Pakistan became an independent nation. Due to its geographical location in South Asia, Pakistan soon became a valuable ally to the United States in its fight against the Soviet Union. Consequently, the U.S. government began to provide economic and military aid to the country. The entry of Pakistan into the British Commonwealth of Nations in 1947 drew the Canadian and Pakistani governments close together, and after 1951, the Canadian government began to inject millions of dollars of development assistance into Pakistan.

Relations between Pakistan and the United States began to falter when Pakistan and India went to war over the disputed region of Jammu and Kashmir in 1965. In protest, the United States suspended military assistance, which generated the widespread feeling in Pakistan that the United States was not a reliable ally. Although military assistance was suspended to both countries involved in the conflict, Pakistan was affected much more severely.

Above: **U.S. secretary of state Dean Rusk** (*far left*)**, U.S. vice president Lyndon Baines Johnson** (*second from left*)**, Pakistani president Mohammad Ayub Khan** (*third from left*)**, and U.S. president John F. Kennedy** (*fourth from left*) **meet at the White House in Washington, D.C., on July 13, 1961.**

Relations gradually improved between Pakistan and the United States, and military aid was resumed in 1975. In April 1979, however, the United States cut off economic aid, except for food assistance, to Pakistan due to concerns about Pakistan's nuclear program.

The Soviet invasion of Afghanistan in December 1979 highlighted the importance of peace and stability in South Asia to both Pakistan and the United States. Due to the increased threat to security in the region and Pakistan's urgent need for economic development, the U.S. government devised a U.S. $3.2 billion military and economic assistance program. The two countries agreed on a second program in 1986, but all military assistance and new economic aid to Pakistan were suspended in 1990 because the country was suspected of continuing its nuclear weapons program.

Pakistan's decision to conduct nuclear tests in May 1998, in response to similar tests carried out by India, soured Pakistani-North American relations. Canada's post-nuclear test measures included suspending all new nonhumanitarian bilateral assistance to Pakistan, while sanctions imposed by the United States restricted military sales, economic assistance, and loans to the Pakistani government.

Left: **Prime Minister Nawaz Sharif (*left*) meets U.S. president Bill Clinton (*right*) in the Oval Office at the White House in Washington, D.C., on December 2, 1998. While Sharif was in power, relations between the United States and Pakistan deteriorated due to the Pakistani government's nuclear weapons program, its pro-Islamic policies, and its alleged support of Islamic fundamentalism.**

Immigration to North America

Pakistani emigration to North America began before the country became an independent nation in 1947. A very small number of people from the area that is now Pakistan arrived in the United States to work on plantations following the abolition of slavery after 1865. The second wave of immigrants from present-day Pakistan began to arrive in the United States at the beginning of the twentieth century. These immigrants were largely uneducated and came to work in mines and orchards and on the railroads. Immigration from modern-day Pakistan and other Asian countries came to an end when the U.S. government passed the Immigration Act of 1924.

Emigration resumed after 1965, when the act was repealed, and the third wave of Pakistani immigrants followed shortly afterward. Further immigration changes also meant that people were given visas based on their ability to contribute to society. As a result, the United States experienced an influx of Pakistani professionals into the country, who were trained to be doctors, educators, scientists, and engineers. In addition, many Pakistanis chose to settle in the United States after completing their studies at American universities and institutes. These groups first settled

REASONS FOR EMIGRATING TO NORTH AMERICA

Over the years, Pakistanis have chosen to settle in North America for a number of reasons. Some have left Pakistan due to recurrent political instability. Others have moved to North America in the hope of finding a better life. Many move because they want their children to have the advantages of a good education system. Having access to a high-quality healthcare system and good job opportunities are also important factors.

Left: Pakistanis arrive in the United States in the late 1960s. The main wave of Pakistani emigration to North America occurred in the mid-1960s, and Pakistanis today have strong communities in the United States and Canada.

Left: **This Pakistani-American works as a computer technician for an electronics company in Chicago.**

in major metropolitan areas, such as New York, Washington, D.C., Chicago, and Houston. The main reasons for flocking to these areas included the availability of jobs, means of transportation, and the existence of small Pakistani communities. These immigrants gradually moved out to suburban areas and have now settled throughout the United States.

Immigration to Canada first began in the early 1900s, when a small number of people from the area that is now the province of Punjab arrived in the country. Within a few years, however, most of these immigrants had either returned to their homeland or made their way to the United States. Immigration stopped after 1907 following an immigration act that prevented South Asians, including those of Muslim or Sikh origin, from entering Canada. In 1967, the Canadian government relaxed the laws on immigration, and Pakistanis began to arrive in greater numbers. As in the United States, these immigrants were well-educated and trained as educators, doctors, engineers, accountants, and scientists. They settled throughout Canada, with the majority establishing themselves in Ontario. Today, Pakistani communities thrive in Canada's large cities, including Vancouver, Toronto, and Montréal.

Current Relations

Both the United States and Canada denounced the Pakistani military coup of October 1999 that brought General Pervez Musharraf to power. Canada led a Commonwealth Ministerial Action Group (CMAG) to Pakistan to encourage an early transition to a democratically elected government; Pakistan's membership to the Commonwealth was subsequently suspended. The United States imposed an additional layer of sanctions, which included restrictions on foreign military financing and economic aid. These sanctions, in combination with previously imposed sanctions, have had a devastating effect on Pakistan's economy.

War on Terrorism

Following the terrorist attacks on the United States on September 11, 2001, Pakistan has agreed to cooperate with the United States and its allies in the effort to end international terrorist activities. The attacks were allegedly led by Saudi Arabian militant Osama bin Laden, who had been living in Afghanistan as a guest of the Taliban government.

In the weeks following the attacks, President Musharraf's government acted as a mediator between the United States and

Left: **U.S. secretary of state Colin Powell (***center***) and Pakistani president General Pervez Musharraf (***right***) stand side by side at a press conference in Islamabad, Pakistan, on October 16, 2001. During their meeting, Powell and Musharraf discussed many issues, including how to begin the process of rebuilding Afghanistan, Pakistan's return to democracy, and broadening U.S.-Pakistan commercial and trade ties.**

Left: U.S. ambassador Wendy Chamberlain (*right*) and Nawid Ahsan, secretary of the Economic Affairs Division of the Ministry of Finance and Economic Affairs in Pakistan (*left*), shake hands after signing a bilateral Paris Club agreement on September 24, 2001, in Islamabad. The agreement will reschedule U.S. $379 million in government-to-government debt in an effort to show U.S. support of Pakistan's economic recovery.

the Taliban and sent a delegation to put pressure on the Afghan government to extradite Osama bin Laden. When these efforts failed, U.S. president George W. Bush announced air strikes against Afghanistan in October 2001. Stressing its support of U.S.-led military action, Pakistan opened its airspace to U.S. warplanes and allowed American forces to use Pakistani air bases for logistics, intelligence gathering, and combat support missions.

The Lifting of Sanctions

North America's policy toward Pakistan changed drastically after the terrorist attacks on the United States. Recognizing the importance of Pakistan's assistance in any action taken against Afghanistan, the United States announced the lifting of separate sets of sanctions imposed on Pakistan in 1979, 1990, and 1998. All these sanctions were related to Pakistan's development of nuclear weapons. The move, however, did not apply to sanctions imposed in 1999 following the military takeover. Pakistan welcomed the move because the country can now receive urgently needed economic aid.

Canada also announced the removal of almost all its economic and political sanctions on Pakistan at the beginning of October 2001 in response to Pakistan's decision to support the U.S.-led campaign against global terrorism. Only the ban on military exports will remain.

U.S. FOREIGN POLICY TOWARD PAKISTAN

During a visit to Pakistan in October 2001, Alan Larson, the U.S. Under Secretary of State for Economic, Business, and Agricultural Affairs, stated that the lifting of sanctions was an important step in improving political and economic relations with Pakistan. Larson also stressed that the move will help the Pakistani government develop a growing economy that will produce benefits and jobs for its people. Nevertheless, U.S. concerns over Pakistan's nuclear program, human rights issues, and development of democracy are still major foreign policy issues.

Humanitarian Ties

Pakistan, the United States, and Canada are members of various organizations, such as the U.N., WHO, and UNESCO, that work to improve the lives of people around the world. These and other international aid agencies are currently sending humanitarian aid to Pakistan as part of the Afghan relief effort, as well as using Pakistan as a base to transport aid into Afghanistan.

Development Agencies

The Canadian International Development Agency (CIDA) is present in Pakistan. The organization focuses on technical, industrial, educational, health, environmental, and social assistance programs. CIDA volunteers are also involved in other community-generated projects, such as increasing awareness of HIV/AIDS.

The U.S. Agency for International Development (USAID) is not currently active in Pakistan. Nevertheless, it does provide assistance to, and through, nongovernmental organizations (NGOs) for humanitarian purposes. Setting up the Pakistan NGO Initiative in 1994, USAID has implemented activities related to economic development, women's and children's health, child labor, and microenterprise development. The initiative is scheduled to end in 2002.

Left: International organizations, such as the United Nations Children's Fund (UNICEF), are supplying urgently needed aid to Pakistan to help the government provide for around two million Afghan refugees living in camps along the Pakistan-Afghanistan border. These refugees have fled their homes in Afghanistan following military strikes by U.S. and British forces in the fight against terrorism.

North Americans in Pakistan

Most North Americans living in Pakistan work in the diplomatic service or are employees of North American companies that have set up offices in the country's major cities. Despite political instability and the country's volatile relationship with India, Pakistan is a popular tourist destination for adventurous North Americans who take advantage of the country's rugged landscape to climb the numerous mountains in the northern and northwestern parts of the country.

North Americans have also contributed to the excavation and preservation of some of Pakistan's historical sites. Numerous volunteers, archaeologists, and art historians have traveled to the country to participate in the excavations of ancient cities, such as Mohenjo-Daro, that date back to the Indus Valley civilization.

Canada and the United States both have embassies in Islamabad. Furthermore, a number of organizations have been set up in the country to promote North American-Pakistani relations. One such institute is the American Center (officially called the Public Affairs Section since 1999) in Lahore. The center fosters the exchange of culture between the Pakistani and North American communities, as well as an understanding of American society.

Above: **This tourist is admiring traditional Pakistani handicrafts in the province of North-West Frontier.**

Left: This Pakistani-American is opening her Pakistani clothes shop in Chicago. Many Pakistani-run businesses in the United States displayed signs, such as the one here, in their shop windows to show their support of U.S-Pakistan unity against terrorism.

Pakistanis in North America

Pakistanis have settled throughout the United States, including New York, Chicago, Los Angeles, and Washington, D.C. About 130,000 Pakistanis make their home in Canada, and vibrant Pakistani communities exist in Ontario, Québec, and British Columbia. Many of these individuals are highly trained professionals who work as doctors, scientists, and engineers.

North America's Pakistani community plays an active role in promoting and nurturing its culture through organizations and committees. Located in Vancouver, the Pakistan-Canada Association aims to retain and enrich the cultural and religious heritage of Pakistani-Canadians. Professional institutions have also been set up throughout North America to provide support for Pakistani professionals who have settled in either the United States or Canada. These organizations, such as the Association of Pakistani Physicians of North America, also participate in medical relief and other charitable activities in both Pakistan and North America. In addition, both a US-Pakistan and Canada-Pakistan Business Council have been set up to expand investment opportunities, trade, and commerce and to enhance business relationships between North America and Pakistan.

Pakistani Influence in North America

Pakistani-North Americans have generally assimilated into North American society, but they still retain their cultural identity by nurturing and fostering aspects of their heritage. Nearly every city with a sizable Pakistani population has restaurants, bakeries, and shops selling Pakistani foods, spices, and goods. Pakistani foods have also found their way into North American cuisine. Creamy curries and Mughal dishes, such as chicken tandoori, are particular favorites, as are the wide array of rich, sugary Pakistani desserts and sweets.

Distinct Pakistani rhythms and beats have made their mark in North American music. Today, musicians from Pakistan and North America collaborate and share styles. Pakistani groups, including Junoon, whose bassist is originally from New York, frequently tour the United States and Canada.

A variety of Pakistani products and handicrafts are becoming increasingly popular with North Americans. These include handwoven carpets. Overseas demand for these goods have affected the designs, and many skilled weavers in Pakistan now concentrate on producing carpets and rugs adorned with intricate Persian patterns in colors attuned to North American tastes.

MOSQUES IN NORTH AMERICA

Religion plays an important role in the lives of many Pakistani-North Americans. Today, the United States has over one thousand mosques, while Canada has fifty-five mosques. These mosques are not only places of worship but also act as centers where Pakistanis gather for other purposes.

Left: Pakistani newspapers and food items are available in this Chicago store, which is owned by a Pakistani-American.

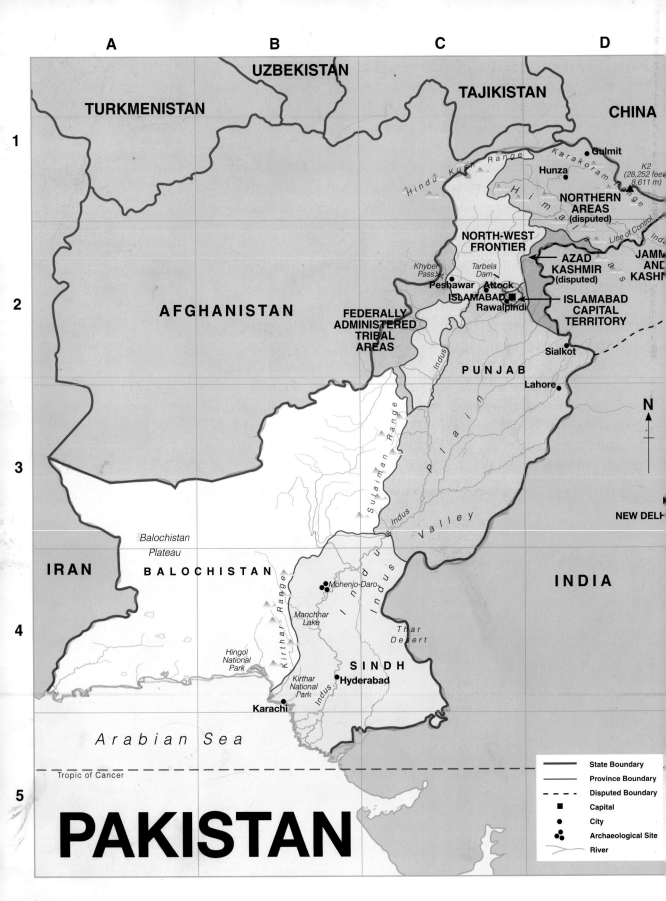

PAKISTAN

86

Above: This man is preparing cakes and sweets to sell at his stall in Peshawar.

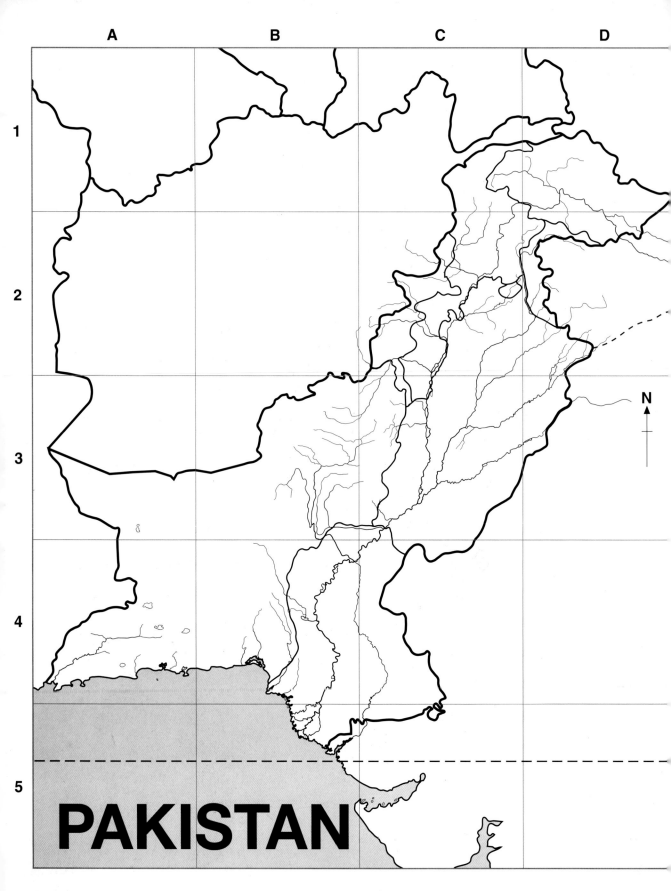

PAKISTAN

88

How Is Your Geography?

Learning to identify the main geographical areas and points of a country can be challenging. Although it may seem difficult at first to memorize the locations and spellings of major cities or the names of mountain ranges, rivers, deserts, lakes, and other prominent physical features, the end result of this effort can be very rewarding. Places you previously did not know existed will suddenly come to life when referred to in world news, whether in newspapers, television reports, other books and reference sources, or on the Internet. This knowledge will make you feel a bit closer to the rest of the world, with its fascinating variety of cultures and physical geography.

Used in a classroom setting, the instructor can make duplicates of this map using a copy machine. (PLEASE DO NOT WRITE IN THIS BOOK!) Students can then fill in any requested information on their individual map copies. Used one-on-one, the student can also make copies of the map on a copy machine and use them as a study tool. The student can practice identifying place names and geographical features on his or her own.

Below: **Traditional music plays an important role at happy occasions celebrated by families, including weddings and the birth of a child. These musicians are performing at a wedding in Hunza.**

Pakistan at a Glance

Official Name   Islamic Republic of Pakistan

Capital   Islamabad

Official Languages   Urdu, English

Population   144,616,639 (July 2001 estimate)

Land Area   310,400 square miles (803,936 square km)

Provinces, *Territory, and **Capital Territory   Balochistan, Federally Administered Tribal Areas*, Islamabad Capital Territory**, North-West Frontier, Punjab, Sindh

Note: The Pakistani-administered section of the disputed Jammu and Kashmir region includes Azad Kashmir and the Northern Areas.

Border Countries   Afghanistan, China, India, Iran

Highest Point   K2 (Mount Godwin-Austen) 28,252 feet (8,611 m)

Major River   Indus

Major Cities   Hyderabad, Islamabad, Karachi, Lahore, Peshawar, Rawalpindi

Ethnic Groups   Baloch, Muhajir, Pashtun, Punjabi, Sindhi

Religions   Islam, Christianity, Hinduism

National Holidays   Pakistan Day (March 23)

Independence Day (August 14)

Defence of Pakistan Day (September 6)

Birth- and death anniversaries of Mohammed Ali Jinnah (December 25 and September 11, respectively)

Religious Festivals   Ramadan, Bakr-Id, Eid ul-Fitr

Major Exports   Cotton, fabrics, rice, yarn

Major Imports   Chemicals, edible oils, flour, grains, machinery, petroleum, petroleum products, transportation equipment

Currency   Pakistan Rupees (61.00 PKR = U.S. $ 1 as of 2001)

Opposite: **This Pakistani villager is wearing a Hunza hat. This type of hat is part of the traditional attire of Pashtuns, who live in both Pakistan and Afghanistan.**

Glossary

(Note: Words followed by an asterisk are common to both Punjabi and Urdu.)

Pashtu Vocabulary

khattak (KHU-tuhk): a sword dance performed by Pashtun men.

pukhtunwali (PUHK-tuhn-wah-lee): the Pashtun code of honor.

Punjabi Vocabulary

baja* (BAH-jah): a harmonium.

bangra (BAHNG-rah): a folk dance that originates from the province of Punjab.

bansari (BAHN-sree): a bamboo or reed flute.

biryani (bir-YAH-nee): rice that is cooked in a meat sauce.

doabs* (doo-WABS): fertile flatlands between the rivers on the Indus Plain that are densely settled and intensively farmed.

kabaddi (kah-buh-DEE): a game that combines wrestling and tag.

lassi (LASS-ee): a drink made from yogurt.

paratha* (puh-RAH-tah): round, flat bread fried in butter.

pattu* (puh-TOO): handwoven woolen cloth.

sag* (SAHG): mustard greens.

sarangi (suh-rung-GEE): a small, stringed instrument with three playing strings that are played with a bow.

Urdu Vocabulary

Bakr-Id (BUK-rah EED): the Muslim Feast of the Sacrifice.

burqa (BOOR-kah): a long garment worn by a Muslim woman that covers her from head to toe.

Eid ul-Fitr (EED OOL-fitr): a festival celebrating the end of Ramadan.

junoon (juh-NOON): passion.

kathak (KUH-tuhk): a north Indian style of classical dance characterized by rhythmic footwork and rapid spins.

mir (MEER): prince.

muhajirs (moo-HAH-jeerz): Muslim immigrants who moved to Pakistan from India at the time of partition in 1947.

qawwal (kah-VAHL): a singer.

qawwali (kah-VAH-lee): a type of Islamic religious music.

rabab (ruh-BAHB): a banjo-like instrument played by plucking the strings.

urs (OORS): festivals that honor Sufi saints.

English Vocabulary

accede: give one's consent by yielding.

accolades: awards; tributes.

agile: quick and well-coordinated in movement.

annexed: incorporated into the domain of a city, country, or state.

appliquéd: having decorations or trimmings made of one material that have been attached to another by sewing or gluing.

arabesques: ornamental styles in which flowers, animals, and other designs are represented in intricate patterns.

autonomy: self-government.

barrages: artificial obstructions in a watercourse that increase the depth of water and facilitate irrigation.

ceded: formally surrendered to another.

conceded: acknowledged as true, just, or proper; admitted, often grudgingly.

coup d'état: unexpected political uprising.

damascening: the art of decorating iron, steel, or bronze by inlaying it with a design in another metal or metals, usually gold or silver.

distributaries: outflowing branches of a stream or river, typically found in a delta.

eclectic: wide-ranging; coming from many different sources.

fable: a story not based on fact; a legend or myth.

flux: continuous change or movement.

frescoes: pictures that are painted on plastered walls when the plaster is wet.

fretted: having ridges of wood, metal, or string set across the fingerboard of an instrument to help the fingers stop the strings at the correct positions.

guerrillas: soldiers who form an unofficial army to fight against an existing political order.

halal: of an animal or its meat slaughtered or prepared in the manner prescribed by Islamic law.

hydroelectricity: the generation of electricity from waterpower.

martial law: law imposed by state military forces in response to civil unrest.

monsoon: a season of heavy rainfall.

muezzin: an announcer, or crier, who calls Muslims to prayer.

pivotal: of vital or crucial importance.

plebiscite: a vote in which the population exercises the right to decide self-rule or affiliation with another country.

portal: a door, gate, or entrance, especially one of imposing size and appearance.

porticoes: structures that consist of roofs supported by columns or piers.

predator: an animal that preys on and kills another animal, usually for food.

pulses: legumes (beans, peas, lentils).

purdah: the seclusion of women from the sight of male nonrelatives or strangers.

resolution: a formal expression of opinion or intention made, usually after voting, by a formal organization.

rosettes: designs that resemble a rose; the compound spots that appear on a leopard.

salinity: relating to the amount of salt contained or present in a body of water, etc.

sanctions: measures taken by a country to restrict trade and official contact with a nation that has broken international law.

socialist: relating to a system in which the production and distribution of goods are owned and controlled collectively or by the government.

stalemate: a situation where no action can be taken or progress made; deadlock.

subcontinent: a large, relatively self-contained landmass that forms the subdivision of a continent

sultanate: territory ruled over by a sultan.

timbre: the characteristic quality of sound produced by an instrument or voice.

vested: placed powers, functions, or rights in the control of someone.

More Books to Read

Hoops of Fire: Fifty Years of Fiction by Pakistani Women. Aamer Hussein, Mumtaz Shirin, and Jamila Hashmi (editors) (Zed Books)

India and the Mughal Empire. Discoveries series. Valerie Berinstain (Harry N. Abrams)

The Indian Subcontinent. Places and People series. Anita Ganeri (Franklin Watts)

K2: Challenging the Sky. Roberto Mantovani and Kurt Diemberger (Mountaineers Books)

Muslim Child. A Collection of Short Stories and Poems. Rukhsana Khan (Napoleon Publishing/Rendezvous Press)

Pakistan. City and Village Life. Country Insights series. Eaniqa Khan and Rob Unwin (Raintree/Steck-Vaughn)

Pakistan. Cultures of the World series. Sean Sheehan (Benchmark Books)

Pakistan. World Focus. Elspeth Clayton (Heinemann)

Pakistan: Major World Nations series. John C. Caldwell (Chelsea House)

Pakistan in Pictures. Visual Geography series. Jon A. Teta (Lerner)

Shabanu: Daughter of the Wind. Suzanne Fisher Staples (Alfred A. Knopf)

Videos

Islam — Empire of Faith. (PBS Home Video)

Mr. Jinnah: The Making of Pakistan. (Christopher Mitchell)

Web Sites

www.geocities.com/RainForest/Jungle/2690/

www.junoon.com

www.pak.gov.pk/

www.storyofpakistan.com/

www.tourism.gov.pk

Due to the dynamic nature of the Internet, some web sites stay current longer than others. To find additional web sites, use a reliable search engine with one or more of the following keywords to help you locate information about Pakistan. Keywords: *Benazir Bhutto, Indus River, Mohammed Ali Jinnah, Junoon, K2, Karachi, Mohenjo-Daro.*

Index